DISEASES AND DISORDERS

BREAST CANCER
RISKS, DETECTION, AND TREATMENT

By Michelle Denton

Portions of this book originally appeared in *Breast Cancer* by Lizabeth Hardman.

Published in 2018 by
Lucent Press, an Imprint of Greenhaven Publishing LLC
353 3rd Avenue
Suite 255
New York, NY 10010

Designer: Deanna Paternostro
Editor: Jennifer Lombardo

Cataloging-in-Publication Data

Names: Denton, Michelle.
Title: Breast cancer: risks, detection, and treatment / Michelle Denton.
Description: New York : Lucent Press, 2018. | Series: Diseases and Disorders | Includes index.
Identifiers: ISBN 9781534562837 (pbk.) | ISBN 9781534561915 (library bound) | ISBN 9781534561908 (ebook)
Subjects: LCSH: Breast–Cancer–Juvenile literature. | Breast–Cancer–Prevention–Juvenile literature.
Classification: LCC RC280.B8 D46 2018 | DDC 616.99'449–dc23

Printed in the United States of America

CPSIA compliance information: Batch #CW18KL: For further information contact Greenhaven Publishing LLC, New York, New York at 1-844-317-7404.

CONTENTS

FOREWORD   4

INTRODUCTION
Struggling and Surviving Together   6

CHAPTER ONE
Breast Cancer 101   12

CHAPTER TWO
Detecting and Diagnosing   27

CHAPTER THREE
Fighting the Good Fight   42

CHAPTER FOUR
Surviving Breast Cancer   56

CHAPTER FIVE
For the Future   76

NOTES   89
GLOSSARY   93
ORGANIZATIONS TO CONTACT   94
FOR MORE INFORMATION   96
INDEX   98
PICTURE CREDITS   103
ABOUT THE AUTHOR   104

FOREWORD

Illness is an unfortunate part of life, and it is one that is often misunderstood. Thanks to advances in science and technology, people have been aware for many years that diseases such as the flu, pneumonia, and chicken pox are caused by viruses and bacteria. These diseases all cause physical symptoms that people can see and understand, and many people have dealt with these diseases themselves. However, sometimes diseases that were previously unknown in most of the world turn into epidemics and spread across the globe. Without an awareness of the method by which these diseases are spread—through the air, through human waste or fluids, through sexual contact, or by some other method—people cannot take the proper precautions to prevent further contamination. Panic often accompanies epidemics as a result of this lack of knowledge.

Knowledge is power in the case of mental disorders, as well. Mental disorders are just as common as physical disorders, but due to a lack of awareness among the general public, they are often stigmatized. Scientists have studied them for years and have found that they are generally caused by hormonal imbalances in the brain, but they have not yet determined with certainty what causes those imbalances or how to fix them. Because even mild mental illness is stigmatized in Western society, many people prefer not to talk about it.

Chronic pain disorders are also not well understood—even by researchers—and do not yet have foolproof treatments. People who have a mental disorder or a disease or disorder that causes them to feel chronic pain can be the target of uninformed opinions. People who do not have these disorders sometimes struggle to understand how difficult it can be to deal with the symptoms. These disorders are often termed "invisible illnesses" because no one can see the symptoms; this leads many people to doubt that they exist or are serious problems. Additionally, people who have an undiagnosed disorder may understand that they are experiencing the world in a different way than their peers, but they have no one to turn to for answers.

Misinformation about all kinds of ailments is often spread through personal anecdotes, social media, and even news sources. This series aims to present accurate information about both physical and mental conditions so young adults will have a better understanding of them. Each volume discusses the symptoms of a particular disease or disorder, ways it is currently being treated, and the research that is being done to understand it further. Advice for people who may be suffering from a disorder is included, as well as information for their loved ones about how best to support them.

With fully cited quotes, a list of recommended books and websites for further research, and informational charts, this series provides young adults with a factual introduction to common illnesses. By learning more about these ailments, they will be better able to prevent the spread of contagious diseases, show compassion to people who are dealing with invisible illnesses, and take charge of their own health.

STRUGGLING AND SURVIVING TOGETHER

Samantha first noticed the lump in her breast while sitting on the couch at her sister's birthday party. At 29 years old, she assumed it was a harmless cyst, a common occurrence in women as they head into their 30s. Nevertheless, she contacted her doctor to have it examined. After test results came back unclear, she went to a general surgeon to have the lump removed, and that was when everything changed. "That day at work, I received a call from the surgeon asking me to call him and saying I should have him paged if he wasn't available," Samantha wrote. "The message alarmed me and I knew something wasn't right. Over the phone, he told me that the lump he'd removed was malignant. I had to clarify what he meant: Was it cancer? When he said the words, 'I'm so sorry,' I knew it was cancer."[1] Samantha's case, however, was relatively unusual. Although breast cancer is the most commonly diagnosed cancer in women in the United States, most breast cancers occur in women over the age of 50.

Breast cancer can affect people of any sex and race. The National Cancer Institute estimated that by the end of 2017, approximately 252,710 cases of breast cancer would be diagnosed in women in the United States and that more than 40,000 of them would die from it. The institute also estimated that more than 2,470 men would develop breast cancer, with about 460 deaths. White women are the most likely to get breast cancer, but black women have the highest death rates after diagnosis, possibly because of genetic differences in the tumors, socioeconomic barriers to getting effective health care, or getting diagnosed at a later stage of the disease. Women who are of Ashkenazi Jewish descent have a higher risk of breast cancer because they tend to carry and pass on a specific genetic mutation that increases breast cancer risk. Hispanic, Asian, and Native American women have the lowest incidence and death rate when it comes to breast cancer, and these occurrences are slowly decreasing.

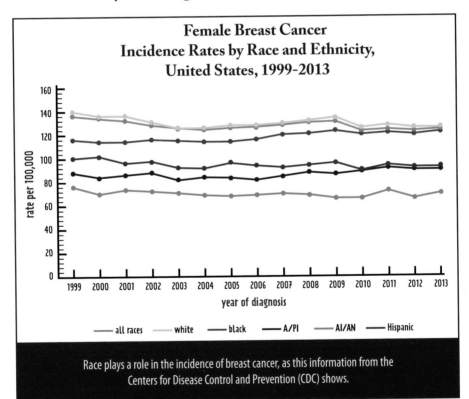

Race plays a role in the incidence of breast cancer, as this information from the Centers for Disease Control and Prevention (CDC) shows.

The overall incidence of breast cancer has been declining since 2000, and death rates from the disease have been decreasing since 1989. Thanks to a greatly improved understanding of the nature of breast cancer and improved treatment methods, the survival rate for some types of breast cancer is nearly 100 percent, especially if it is detected early.

Historically Speaking

Breast cancer is one of the oldest known forms of cancer in humans. The Edwin Smith Papyrus, an Egyptian text that dates back to about 1600 BC, mentions eight cases of tumors, or masses, of the breast and states that there was no treatment for it. It was not until the 17th century, when doctors learned of the relationship between cancer and the lymphatic system through which cancer spreads, that treatment methods began to develop. Surgeons in France and Scotland in the 18th century were among the first to treat breast cancer with a mastectomy—the surgical removal of the breast—along with the chest wall muscle underneath it and the lymph nodes in the axilla, or armpit.

Renowned American surgeon William Halsted began performing mastectomies in 1882. His radical procedure often involved removing both breasts, along with the chest muscles and axillary lymph nodes on both sides. The procedure commonly left the woman disabled and in a great deal of pain, and there was no medical or scientific evidence that the procedure actually resulted in a higher cure rate. Despite these drawbacks, the procedure remained in use even into the 1980s. As one woman put it, after her radical mastectomy in 1971, "I went to the hospital feeling perfectly healthy, and came out grotesquely mutilated—a mental and physical wreck."[2]

In the late 1970s, with a more complete understanding of breast cancer and how it spreads, surgeries were developed that spared the chest wall muscles and often the lymph nodes in the armpit. A radical mastectomy became less common in favor of the

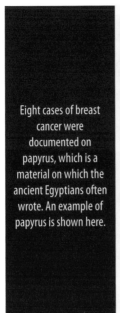

Eight cases of breast cancer were documented on papyrus, which is a material on which the ancient Egyptians often wrote. An example of papyrus is shown here.

tissue-sparing lumpectomy, which removes only the part of the breast that contains the cancer. "That particular advance is an enormous benefit because of the improved quality of life and improved self-image," said Dr. Lawrence Solin, a professor in radiation oncology at the University of Pennsylvania's Perelman School of Medicine. "There are better outcomes all the way around."[3]

Finding Understanding and Hope

Despite these drastic improvements in breast cancer detection and treatment, a diagnosis of breast cancer can still be cause for a great deal of fear and anxiety. Until the middle of the 20th century, cancer was not openly discussed. "Cancer was a word that was whispered," wrote Betty Ford, wife of President Gerald Ford. Betty's breast cancer was diagnosed in 1974. "If somebody had cancer, and particularly breast cancer, it was a topic that people covered up and only whispered about behind their hand so no one would hear it."[4]

Lack of knowledge about cancer meant a diagnosis of the disease would almost certainly result in death, and people feared cancer above all other diseases. Because breast cancer affects many more women than men, and because doctors and patients often felt uncomfortable talking about a woman's breasts, many women delayed seeking medical attention, even when the cancer was far advanced. Many people considered it to be the woman's own fault if she got breast cancer—that women who lived pure and healthy lives would not get such a "shameful" disease.

Since the 1970s, however, attitudes about discussing breasts have become much more open. High-profile women, such as Ford; former Supreme Court justice Sandra Day O'Connor; WNBA player Edna Campbell; and actresses Shirley Temple, Jill Eikenberry, and more recently, Angelina Jolie took their struggles with breast cancer and breast health public, which increased awareness of breast cancer and decreased the negative assumptions about the women who got it. As Ford wrote, "It was a real awakening for the women of the United States to have the wife of the president have breast cancer and speak of it ... People were shocked and yet they became more open about addressing the issue."[5]

In 2013, actress Angelina Jolie announced that she had undergone a preventative double mastectomy, bringing the public's attention to the role of genetics in breast cancer.

Since that time, women have become more comfortable talking about their own bodies. Also, having more women in the medical profession means women who are hesitant to see a male doctor can choose a female doctor instead. This feeling of comfort may encourage women to seek medical attention sooner. "I remember when you couldn't even say 'breast,' let alone 'breast cancer,'" said Fran Visco, president of the National Breast Cancer Coalition. "That has changed quite a bit. Even if you have breast cancer, you are still full of life."[6] Dr. Solin added, "There has been enormous improvement in our ability to detect it early, and treat and cure patients. We have had a dramatic reduction in mortality, and the treatments are more effective."[7] Increased awareness of women's health issues, coupled with medical advances, has provided women with options for treatment to actively fight the disease with a realistic hope for survival.

CHAPTER ONE

BREAST CANCER 101

All the parts of the human body are made up of cells. Cells are like highly specialized building blocks; liver cells build a liver, heart cells build a heart, skin cells build the skin, and so on. In the nucleus, or center, of each cell are 23 pairs of chromosomes, and each chromosome is made up of microscopic structures called genes. Genes are the instructions used by the cells to regulate their creation, growth, and death. In a healthy body, cells age and die off in a process called apoptosis, and they are replaced with new cells in an orderly, controlled fashion. When damage occurs, such as when a person gets a cut in the skin, the genes instruct the cells involved to grow faster to replace the damaged tissue. When the damage is healed, the genes tell the cells to slow down and return to their normal rate of growth.

Sometimes, however, the normal genetic mechanism that tells cells when to stop growing malfunctions because of errors, or mutations, in the genes, and normal apoptosis does not take place. Nurse practitioner Rosalind Benedet explained, "Unlike normal cells, which divide a limited number of times before they die, these mutated cells have become 'immortal'—they never stop dividing. One cell divides into two, two divide into four, and so on, and this mass of cells forms a tumor."[8] A tumor is a lump, or mass, of abnormal cells.

Some tumors are harmless. They grow to a certain size and then typically stop growing, and they tend to grow in only one place. These harmless tumors are referred to as benign tumors. A lipoma, made of fat cells, is an example of a benign tumor that grows under the skin. A fibroma is a benign tumor made of connective tissue that can show up in any part of the body. Skin tags and keloid scars are examples of skin fibromas. Some benign tumors can grow very large and may cause discomfort if they press on internal organs or nerves, and they may be unpleasant-looking if they grow on a visible part of the body. If a benign tumor creates problems for the person who has it, it can generally be surgically removed with no harm done. Benign tumors are not cancerous.

Cell Damage and Mutations

Apoptosis is controlled by the deoxyribonucleic acid (DNA) in the nucleus of the cell; DNA is the genetic material that provides all the instructions to the cell about what its function is and how it is supposed to behave.

Damage to the DNA of a cell causes errors, or mutations, in the DNA, which causes the cell to malfunction. Normally, cells either repair the damage or die. If enough mutations occur in the DNA because of the damage, however, the cell may lose its ability to repair itself and also lose the ability to die off. Instead, it may begin to grow and divide out of control, creating more and more cells with the damaged DNA instructions. Cancer cells never mature into the kind of tissue they were supposed to become, they do not stay in one place, and they do not respond to instructions from other cells.

Damage to DNA is most often caused by something the person is exposed to in the environment. People can help minimize their chances of getting cancer by avoiding carcinogens—things that are known to damage DNA and cause cancer. Common carcinogens include: tobacco in all its forms; ultraviolet (UV) radiation from sun exposure or tanning beds; toxic industrial chemicals such as pesticides, vinyl chloride, and asbestos; and some viruses, including HPV, the human papilloma virus.

What Cancer Is

A cancerous tumor is also an abnormal growth of cells in a particular organ or tissue type, but unlike benign tumors, cancerous tumors are potentially harmful to the individual that has one. There are several different classes of cancer types. Breast cancer is of the class called carcinomas, which are cancers that occur in skin tissue or the lining of the internal organs. Cancerous tumors are malignant, and unlike benign tumors, they do not stop growing. Another important difference is that cancerous cells can leave the original tumor and spread to other parts of the body. Once there, the cells can grow and create new tumors. When

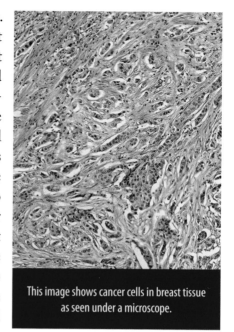

This image shows cancer cells in breast tissue as seen under a microscope.

cancer cells migrate to another part of the body and start to grow there, the process is called metastasis. A cancer that spreads to another organ is referred to by the organ from which it started. For example, breast cancer that has spread to the thyroid is called metastatic breast cancer, not thyroid cancer. Cancers that metastasize to another body organ can devastate the body, can alter treatment plans, and are more deadly than cancers that do not metastasize.

Causes of Death

There are several ways cancer can kill its victim. If the cancer is located inside a vital organ, it can interfere with the function of that organ. For example, a brain tumor can grow large enough that it presses on delicate brain tissue, leading to coma and eventual death. A tumor in the lung can block air passages and cause respiratory failure.

Most cancer deaths, however, are not caused by the primary, or main, tumor. They are caused when cells from the primary tumor metastasize to other organs and grow there. A common example is colon cancer. Colon cancer by itself does not generally cause death, but when it spreads, it tends to spread to the liver, a vital organ. Eventually, the colon cancer cells replace so much liver tissue that the patient dies from liver failure. Breast cancer most commonly spreads to the lungs, liver, brain, and bones.

Another way cancer causes death is through tumor burden, which is related to the amount of tumor tissue containing cancerous cells in the body. The rapid growth and multiplication of cancer cells requires a great deal of energy. Cancer cells take for themselves much of the body's energy sources and proteins that are needed for building healthy tissues. They do this by creating their own blood vessels in a process called angiogenesis. In addition, cancers tend to produce large amounts of chemicals called cytokines. Cytokines are normally produced in small amounts in areas of injury, but the abnormal amounts produced by cancers severely disrupt the body's normal functions. These two characteristics of cancer cells cause many cancer patients to lose a lot of weight, become very weak, and look as if they are "wasting away"—a condition called cachexia. The more the cancer spreads, the higher the tumor burden becomes, and the more cachectic the patient becomes. As the patient weakens, their body becomes unable to combat even minor infections. Death can come from illnesses such as pneumonia— an infection of the lungs—and sepsis—an infection in the blood. Tumor burden is the most common way breast cancer causes death.

The Breast's Anatomy

The human breast is a gland. Glands are organs that produce and secrete substances needed by the body. For example, sweat glands secrete sweat. The pancreas secretes insulin for metabolizing sugar. The breast secretes milk for feeding infants. The breast is made up mostly of fatty tissue and breast tissue. These tissues are what give the breast its size and shape, depending mostly on genetic factors. Nerves, small veins, and small arteries run through the breast. Everything is held together with connective tissue. The breast has no muscle of its own (except for some very tiny muscles around the nipple), but right behind the breast and in front of the ribs is the pectoralis muscle, the main muscle of the chest.

Breast tissue is made up of a system of lobules and ducts. Lobules are clusters of very small sacs that look like tiny grapes. They are lined with special cells that produce milk. Each breast has about 12 to 15 lobules. Ducts are tiny tubes that carry the milk from the lobules out of the breast through the nipple during breastfeeding. Ducts from the lobules join together into larger ducts, eventually ending in about 5 to 10 ducts that end at the nipple. Around the nipple is a circular pigmented area called the areola. The areola secretes small amounts of fluid during breastfeeding to help keep the nipple lubricated.

Also running through the breast are tiny vessels called lymphatic vessels. They carry a clear fluid called lymph that filters out bacteria and waste products of cell metabolism as well as any other foreign substances that may get into the bloodstream. Lymph also contains immune system cells, such as white blood cells that help fight off infections. Lymphatic vessels lead to lymph nodes—small, bean-shaped structures that are part of the immune system. Lymph nodes collect and concentrate the unwanted materials in the lymph so immune system cells can eliminate them from the body.

Lymph nodes are found throughout the body, but chains or clusters of lymph nodes are especially numerous in the neck, the armpit, and the groin

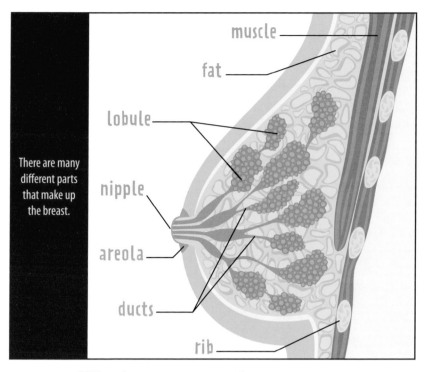

muscle

fat

lobule

There are many different parts that make up the breast.

nipple

areola

ducts

rib

area. When breast cancer spreads, it is most commonly through lymphatic vessels. Breast cancer cells can enter the lymphatic vessels and travel to the lymph nodes. From there, they can get into the bloodstream and travel to other parts of the body.

Lobular and Ductal Breast Cancer

Breast cancers may be described in one of two main ways, depending on the part of the breast in which they begin. The first type is called lobular carcinoma. As its name suggests, lobular carcinomas arise in the lobules. About 15 percent of breast cancers are lobular carcinomas. The more common type is ductal carcinoma. Ductal carcinomas arise in the ducts. They account for about 85 percent of breast cancers.

Another important distinction concerns whether or not the cancer has spread outside the breast. Breast cancer that has not yet spread is called carcinoma in situ.

The term "in situ" means "in place." These are cancers that have not yet left the lobules or the ducts where they began. For this reason, carcinoma in situ is often considered a precancerous, or noninvasive, condition. A woman may have ductal carcinoma in situ (DCIS) or lobular carcinoma in situ (LCIS). DCIS is the most common form of noninvasive breast cancer, and almost all women with this kind can be cured. LCIS is not a true cancer because it does not grow through the wall of the lobules, but women with LCIS do have an increased risk of developing the more serious invasive carcinoma.

Invasive, or infiltrating, carcinoma is a cancer that has already spread outside of the duct or lobule and into the surrounding breast tissue. Once in the breast tissue, it can leave the breast via the lymphatic vessels and nodes and metastasize to other organs. Eighty percent of all invasive breast cancers are invasive ductal carcinoma (IDC), 10 percent are invasive lobular carcinoma (ILC), and the rest are other types of breast cancer.

Other Breast Cancers

Besides IDC and ILC, there are several other, less common types of breast cancer. One example is medullary carcinoma, a form of IDC that gets its name from its color, which is similar to tissue in the brain called the medulla. It represents only about 3 to 5 percent of all breast cancers. Its cells are very large, and medullary tumors are very distinctive from the normal breast tissue around them. It is somewhat fast-growing but does not tend to spread to the lymph nodes as quickly as other invasive forms of breast cancer. Medullary carcinoma can generally be treated successfully.

Another less common type of breast cancer is inflammatory breast cancer (IBC). IBC is a very serious and aggressive form of breast cancer, but it is even less common than medullary carcinoma, accounting for only about 1 to 3 percent of breast cancers. It tends to affect younger women more than other types do. It first shows up with swelling, redness, pain, and warmth in the breast. The skin begins to look thick and bumpy, like the skin of an orange. This sign is called *peau d'orange*, which is French for "orange peel skin." Inflammatory breast cancer may be hard to diagnose at first because it is uncommon and does not show up well on X-rays. Additionally, the symptoms are similar to an infection of the breast called mastitis. Inflammatory breast cancer may be suspected if the symptoms do not respond to antibiotics and if there is no fever present.

A third example is Paget's disease of the nipple, which accounts for 2 to 5 percent of all breast cancers. In almost all cases of Paget's disease, the woman already has another form of breast cancer, such as DCIS or IDC. The cause of Paget's disease is not clear, but one theory is that certain cancer cells, called Paget cells, break off from the main tumor and move through the milk ducts to the skin of the nipple and areola. Because the early symptoms are minor—including redness, itching, and some flaking of the skin—it is often undiagnosed until the underlying cancer is found.

Stages of Breast Cancer

After the type of breast cancer has been determined, a further way to describe and classify it is by its stage. "Patience is important here, for both the woman and her physician," warned cancer specialists Dr. Yashar Hirshaut and Dr. Peter I. Pressman. "The reason a precise identification is important is that these are the factors that affect risk and that make it possible to determine what ought to be done to treat the patient most effectively."[9] Staging also helps doctors and their patients get a better idea of the prognosis—how well the patient is likely to respond to the treatment methods and what the most likely outcome of treatment will be. It also provides a standardized way for breast cancers to be described so treatment results and outcomes can be shared with other doctors, and so doctors and researchers everywhere can have consistent understanding when it comes to studying and learning about breast cancer.

The stage of a breast cancer depends on its size, its location in the breast, whether it is invasive or noninvasive, whether or not lymph nodes are involved, and whether or not it has spread to other organs. Stage 0 is a noninvasive DCIS or LCIS, which has not spread outside of the duct or lobule. Stage I is an invasive cancer that has spread outside the duct or lobule but has not spread to the lymph nodes and is less than 2 cm in size. (Medical professionals measure all tumors in centimeters.)

Stage II cancers are further divided into IIA and IIB. Stage IIA describes tumors in which cancer cells have spread to the lymph nodes in the armpit or situations in which there are no cancer cells in the nodes but the tumor is between 2 and 5 cm in size. Stage IIB means the tumor is between 2 and 5 cm and has spread to the lymph nodes or that the tumor has not yet spread to

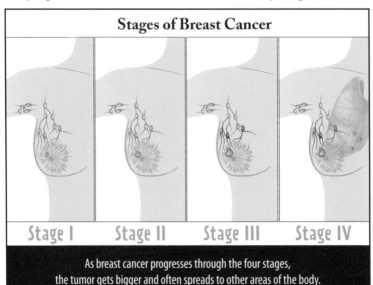

Stages of Breast Cancer

Stage I   Stage II   Stage III   Stage IV

As breast cancer progresses through the four stages, the tumor gets bigger and often spreads to other areas of the body.

the nodes but is larger than 5 cm in size.

Stage III is divided into three substages labeled IIIA, IIIB, and IIIC. In Stage III cancers, the tumor may be larger than 5 cm in size. The axillary nodes test positive for cancer cells, and these cells have begun to clump together or stick to other structures in the axilla. There may also be cancer cells in the nodes near the breastbone, or they may have spread to other areas of the chest wall or to the skin of the breast.

In Stage IV breast cancer, the cancer has metastasized to other organs in the body. Sometimes the breast tumor is not found before it metastasizes and the diagnosis of breast cancer comes later, when the metastatic tumor causes symptoms in the other part of the body.

Survival Rates

Staging breast cancer is very important because it helps doctors provide information to the patient about their prognosis. When oncologists—doctors who specialize in cancer—talk about treatment, they often speak in terms of "five-year relative survival rate." This refers to the percentage of people with a given type of cancer who are still living at least five years after diagnosis of the cancer. Survival rates for different kinds of cancer are determined based on the experiences of thousands of other people who have been diagnosed with the same kind of cancer at the same stage. Statistics about survival rates cannot predict what will happen to an individual patient, however, because each person's situation—the stage of their cancer, other health problems, access to medical care, and many other factors—is unique to that particular patient.

Survival rates vary depending on the type of cancer involved and, more importantly, the stage at which it is diagnosed. Generally speaking, the earlier the cancer is diagnosed and treated, the better the survival rate.

According to the American Cancer Society, for most breast cancers, those who are at Stage 0 or I when diagnosed have a relative survival rate of nearly 100 percent. This means that out of 100 women diagnosed at Stage 0 or Stage I, almost all of them can expect to be living at least 5 years after diagnosis. Stage II cancers have an approximately 93 percent 5-year relative survival rate. Stage III cancers have a relative survival rate of about 72 percent, and the relative survival rate for Stage IV is about 22 percent. An exception to this is inflammatory breast cancer (IBC). Because IBC is very aggressive and is more likely to have metastasized by the time it is diagnosed, IBC is almost always at Stage IIIB or IV at the time of diagnosis. The five-year relative survival rate for IBC depends on the type of treatment. Patients who receive radiation, chemotherapy, and surgery have a 55 percent relative survival rate; those who receive only chemotherapy and surgery have a relative survival rate of 43 percent; and those who receive surgery and radiation therapy have a 41 percent relative survival rate. A patient's ability to receive multiple types of treatment often depends on their health insurance coverage, the amount of money they make, and whether they live in an area where all three options are available.

Risk Factors

It is not fully understood what makes cancer start in some people and not others, but there are several risk factors that may make it more likely that a person will develop breast cancer. The most important are gender and age. Both men and women have breast tissue, but women are approximately 100 times more likely than men to get breast cancer. This is partly because they have more breast tissue, but more importantly, women produce much more of a hormone called estrogen, which is known to support the growth of some kinds of breast cancer.

The risk of breast cancer increases with age. As people grow older, the normal wear and tear of aging can cause genes to mutate, which can affect the normal process of apoptosis. Genetic abnormalities that occur because of the normal aging process are responsible for 90 percent of breast cancers. Most advanced cases of breast cancer—about two out of three—are seen in women over the age of 55. About 10 percent are caused by genetic mutations inherited from a parent.

Genetic Inheritance

Genetic mutations can occur because of aging, but they can also be inherited, or passed down, from parent to child. About 20 to 30 percent of women with breast cancer have a first-degree relative—a mother, sister, or daughter—who has been diagnosed with it. The risk is higher if the relative was diagnosed before age 40.

The most common inherited mutations are called BRCA1 and BRCA2 (for BReast CAncer), discovered in 1994. Normal BRCA genes work by making proteins that fix mutations in other genes. Cells with abnormal BRCA genes cannot fix mutations, including those in another gene called PTEN. PTEN is a tumor suppression gene. It makes cancer cells stop growing. Dr. Ramon Parsons explained what happens when there is a BRCA mutation: "If a cut occurs in PTEN, there is no way for the cell to fix it. It is like cutting the brake on a cable car. If PTEN is broken, you turn on a pathway that tells the cells to grow. It tells the cell to start dividing. It tells the cell, 'don't die.'"[10] Abnormal BRCA genes are unable to fix mutated PTEN, so it cannot

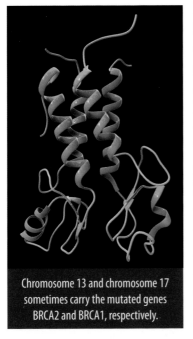

Chromosome 13 and chromosome 17 sometimes carry the mutated genes BRCA2 and BRCA1, respectively.

stop tumor cell growth. Women with mutations in the BRCA genes have about a 60 percent chance of getting breast cancer at some time in their lives, and they are more likely to develop it earlier—under age 50.

Health History

Women who start their menstrual periods early in life—before age 12—or stop having periods late—after age 50—are also at a higher risk of developing breast cancer. This is because they are exposed to more estrogen over their lifetimes, which has been linked to increased risk of breast cancer. Women who have children before age 30 are at a lower risk because early pregnancy causes changes in breast tissue that seem to help protect it from becoming cancerous.

Women with a previous diagnosis of breast cancer have a three to four times higher risk of developing a new cancer in the other breast or in another part of the same breast. Women who have had radiation treatment for other kinds of cancer also have a higher risk, especially if the radiation was given during adolescence, when the breast tissue was developing. Women who, in the 1940s through the 1960s, received a synthetic form of estrogen called DES to help prevent miscarriage may have an increased risk, and their female children may also have a slightly increased risk.

Lifestyle Factors

Gender, age, and heredity are risk factors for breast cancer that a person has no control over. There are other risk factors, however, that can be controlled. Rosy Daniel, author of *The Cancer Prevention Book*, believes controllable risk factors are incredibly important. "Just like heart disease," she wrote, "cancer is primarily a lifestyle-related disease. This means that if we change our lifestyle and habits, we can considerably reduce our risk of getting cancer."[11]

There is evidence that alcohol consumption may increase the risk of getting cancer. According to a very large study done from 1996 to 2001 in the United Kingdom (UK), called the Million Women Study, even small amounts of daily alcohol consumption increased the risk of several kinds of cancer, but the biggest increase in risk was related to breast cancer. The study found that for every 10 grams (about one-third of an ounce or 10 cc) of alcohol consumed per day, the risk of developing breast cancer went up by 12 percent, regardless of the type of alcohol consumed. Another study, published in 2009, found that women who have 14 or more alcoholic drinks of any kind per week are 24 percent more likely to get breast cancer compared to women who do not drink. The reason for the increased risk is not yet clear, but researchers think it may be related to alcohol's effect on the way the body metabolizes estrogen.

Breast Cancer: A Man's Problem, Too

Both boys and girls have some breast tissue in childhood, but when boys reach puberty, changes in their hormone levels—including increased levels of testosterone and decreased levels of estrogen—prevent development of any significant amount of breast tissue. They may have a few underdeveloped ducts, but essentially, they have no lobules in their breasts. Because of this, breast cancer in men is generally ductal carcinoma.

The American Cancer Society estimates that as many as 2,400 men will get breast cancer in 2017. "Even though we don't think of men as having breasts, they have breast tissue and are susceptible to getting breast cancer," said Dr. Sharon Giordano of the M.D. Anderson Cancer Institute in Dallas, Texas. "All men have some degree of residual breast tissue behind the nipples. It may be very small, but just like any part of the body can get cancer, that part of the body can get cancer."[1]

Men who have a genetic condition called Kleinfelter's syndrome are at increased risk for getting breast cancer because men with this condition produce more estrogen than other men. Men with BRCA1 or BRCA2 mutations are also at increased risk for developing breast cancer by age 70. There is a 1 percent risk for men with BRCA1 and a 6 percent risk for men with BRCA2. As with women, other risk factors for male breast cancer include obesity, smoking, and alcoholism.

1. Quoted in Madison Park, "Original KISS Drummer Celebrates Surviving Breast Cancer," CNN, 2008. www.cnn.com/2009/HEALTH/10/15/male.breast.cancer/index.html.

Other lifestyle choices that may affect breast cancer risk include smoking, diet, weight, and physical activity. Smoking increases the risk of many kinds of cancer because the many toxins in cigarette smoke damage the genetic material inside the cells. A diet that is high in cholesterol and fat, especially animal fats, is associated with increased risk of several types of cancer, including breast cancer. Eating a lot of red meat and processed meats such as bacon and sausage may contribute to this risk because they may contain hormones, pesticides, or antibiotics that can damage cells. Obesity, especially later in life, is also associated with greater risk of breast cancer because fat is the main source of estrogen after menopause, the time in a woman's life when her ovaries stop producing it. Regular physical activity, especially in young adulthood, can help decrease the risk of breast cancer because it helps keep body weight under control.

Studies suggest that smoking increases an individual's risk of developing several different kinds of cancers, including breast cancer.

Breast tissue is very sensitive to these kinds of controllable risk factors. They may all trigger that first cell to become a cancer cell and change a woman's life. Despite the number of known risk factors for breast cancer, however, most women with the disease have no risk factors other than their sex or their age.

CHAPTER TWO

DETECTING AND DIAGNOSING

In the past, the first diagnosable sign of breast cancer was the lumps associated with the disease. By the time these tumors were big enough to be felt with the human hand, the cancer had often already spread to other parts of the body, and many women died because there was no way to detect breast cancer earlier. It was not until the early part of the 20th century that the mammogram—a method of screening using X-rays to see inside the breast—was invented, and it was not until the 1960s that research showed that mammograms decreased the mortality rate of breast cancer by about one-third. Another decade passed before mammograms became part of standard practice, and even then, women had to fight to bring breast cancer into the public eye because it had been considered a shameful secret for most of human history.

In 1982, an organization called the Susan G. Komen Breast Cancer Foundation was established in memory of Susan G. Komen, who died of breast cancer in 1980 at the age of 36. Since its creation, it has invested more than $2 billion into breast cancer research, education, and support for breast cancer patients and their families. Largely because of efforts such as this, a great deal has been learned about breast cancer and its treatment, and women are much more aware of the need for early diagnosis of this disease. Today, most breast cancers are discovered at a much earlier stage than they were 30 years ago, and generally before any symptoms appear. However, many cases still go undiagnosed until symptoms appear and the woman seeks medical attention.

Early Warning Signs

The most common early sign of breast cancer is a thickening or lump felt in or around the breast or the axilla. A lump that is painless and feels hard with uneven edges is more likely to be cancer; however, it may also be breast cancer when a mass feels soft and rounded and possibly painful. An important exception to this is inflammatory breast cancer, which does not form lumps but grows in a sheet-like pattern and invades the skin of the breast.

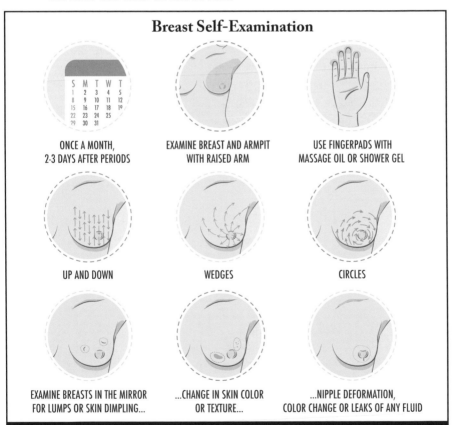

Breast Self-Examination

ONCE A MONTH, 2-3 DAYS AFTER PERIODS

EXAMINE BREAST AND ARMPIT WITH RAISED ARM

USE FINGERPADS WITH MASSAGE OIL OR SHOWER GEL

UP AND DOWN

WEDGES

CIRCLES

EXAMINE BREASTS IN THE MIRROR FOR LUMPS OR SKIN DIMPLING...

...CHANGE IN SKIN COLOR OR TEXTURE...

...NIPPLE DEFORMATION, COLOR CHANGE OR LEAKS OF ANY FLUID

Monthly breast self-exams to check for changes in the appearance or feel of the breast and nipple are important in detecting breast cancer early.

Another early sign is a change in the size or shape of the breast. James, a British man who developed breast cancer in his late 40s, discovered his cancer this way. He said, "I was in the gym changing room and glanced across at a mirror. I noticed that my chest looked a little unbalanced, that the right side appeared bigger. When I had a closer look, there was a lump about the size of a fifty pence piece [slightly larger than a quarter] to the left of my right nipple. It felt hard to the touch. Of course, it never occurred to me that I might have breast cancer. How wrong I was."[12]

Changes in the look or feel of the nipple are also important signs of possible breast cancer. There may be a discharge of blood or fluid from the nipple. The fluid may be clear, or it may be whitish or yellowish in color. The nipple may also become inverted, or turned inward, looking as if it has sunken into the breast. Many of these symptoms can be caused by other, non-cancerous conditions such as infections or hormonal changes, but any changes in the breast should always be brought to the attention of a doctor.

Tests for Breast Cancer

Tests related to breast cancer fall into three main categories—screening, diagnostic, and monitoring. Screening tests are given to healthy people who do not show signs of cancer. "A screening test tries to find a disease before there are any symptoms," said Dr. Susan G. Orel, a professor of radiology. "With breast cancer, there's a misconception that if you feel fine, don't have a lump, and have no family history of breast cancer, you're okay. The truth is that three quarters of the women in whom we find breast cancer have no risk factors. So screening is important for everyone."[13]

Diagnostic tests are given to women who have either developed symptoms of breast cancer or whose screening test has turned up an area of suspicion. These tests either rule out breast cancer or they confirm it and help doctors decide on a course of treatment. Monitoring tests are done during and after breast cancer treatment. They help doctors evaluate the effectiveness of treatment and check for recurrences and metastasis.

Screening with Mammograms

By far, the most common screening test for breast cancer is the mammogram. A mammogram is an X-ray of the breast that uses a low dose of radiation to create an image of the inside of the breast. Mammograms can detect several abnormalities. For example, calcifications—tiny grain-like pieces of calcium in the breast tissue—can sometimes be a sign of an early breast cancer before a lump can be felt. Mammograms can also detect cysts—fluid-filled masses that are almost never cancerous—and fibroadenomas, which are very common benign breast masses.

Mammograms have been in use since the mid-1960s. "Mammography plays a critical part in diagnosing breast cancer," said Orel. "In the past, we'd often find that a woman had breast cancer when she came in with a lump. Today, the cancers radiologists

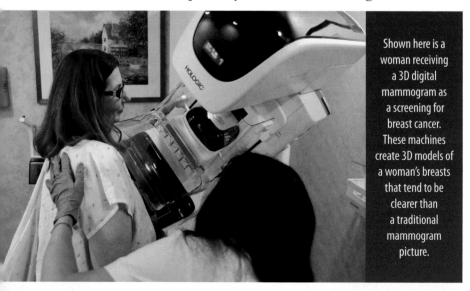

Shown here is a woman receiving a 3D digital mammogram as a screening for breast cancer. These machines create 3D models of a woman's breasts that tend to be clearer than a traditional mammogram picture.

find on mammography are usually detected early, before they can be felt by the patient, are smaller than cancers felt by patients, and have much lower levels of lymph node involvement."[14] Mammograms have been shown to decrease the risk of dying from breast cancer by as much as 35 percent in women over 50. Most cancer experts recommend that women over 40 (younger if the woman is at high risk) get a screening mammogram once a year. In the past, mammogram results were printed out onto X-ray film, but today, most mammograms are digital.

During mammography, a technician positions the breast between two clear plates, which are connected to a specialized camera. The plates are brought together, which gently compresses the breast to spread out and reduce the thickness of the tissue so a more accurate image is obtained. Images are taken in two directions—from top to bottom and from side

Using Computer Technology

Computer-aided detection and diagnosis, or CAD, is a method of using specialized computer software to focus very closely on a particular area of concern found on a digital mammogram. The CAD software can highlight areas of concern with markers right on the viewing screen.

CAD has been available since 1998, but early research into its effectiveness at making more accurate readings of mammograms did not show a clear advantage. There was no clear evidence that CAD provided more accurate readings than having a second radiologist read the mammogram. Additionally, a possible disadvantage of CAD was its tendency to render a reading that interpreted normal changes as possible cancers—a "false positive" reading—that led to more tests and even surgery where no cancer existed. A 2007 study of more than 220,000 women showed that those who got their mammograms done at facilities that had CAD technology were more likely to have their mammograms read as abnormal and then had to have a biopsy to rule out cancer. Recently, however, CAD has proven to detect cancer earlier than mammograms alone, so doctors and software engineers have begun trying to reduce the risk of false positives by adding steps to CAD's diagnostic procedure to double-check its findings. With these extra steps in place, CAD could become a much more reliable tool in the fight against breast cancer in the next few years.

to side—and uploaded directly to a computer. The compression can be somewhat uncomfortable, but it takes only a few seconds to take the images, and the entire procedure takes about 20 minutes.

Breast Exams and Early Detection

Another screening test that is also valuable for catching breast cancer early is the breast exam, done either by a doctor or by the woman herself. A clinical breast exam is done by a doctor in the office during the woman's routine, yearly physical examination. The doctor checks for any changes in the size or shape of the breasts and for changes in the skin or the nipple. Then, using small, circular motions around the entire surface of the breast, the doctor gently presses, or palpates, to make sure there are no masses in the breast tissue or fluid discharge from the nipples. The doctor will also palpate the axilla and the area under the collarbone to check for enlarged lymph nodes.

Breast self-exam (BSE) is very similar to the clinical exam except that it is done at home by the woman. During BSE, the woman looks in the mirror to check for the same signs the doctor does during a clinical breast exam. She then lies down and checks her breasts and armpits for lumps, using the fingertips to palpate the entire surface. Many women have found their own breast cancers before they were seen on a mammogram. Most doctors recommend that women do BSE at least once a month, in addition to having a yearly clinical exam.

Ultrasonography

Ultrasound is a commonly used diagnostic tool. It uses high-frequency sound waves—too high to be detected by the human ear. The ultrasound technician moves a special probe over the area of the breast to be examined.

The probe sends the sound waves into the breast. The sound waves bounce back off the tissue at different rates, depending on the density of the tissue with which they come in contact. The ultrasound machine converts the reflected sound waves into an image on a screen. The best use of a breast ultrasound is to determine if a mass in the breast is solid or if it is a fluid-filled cyst. A solid tumor will appear whitish on the screen, but a cyst will appear black because the sound waves travel right through fluid rather than reflecting off of it.

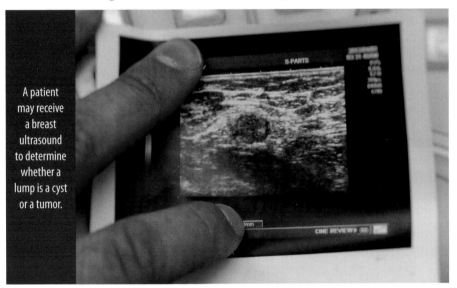

A patient may receive a breast ultrasound to determine whether a lump is a cyst or a tumor.

Biopsy: Getting Physical Proof

Imaging tests such as mammograms and ultrasounds, along with physical breast exams, may raise the suspicion of breast cancer, but they cannot absolutely confirm the diagnosis. The only way to do this is to take a biopsy—a sample of the tissue in the area of concern—and examine it under a microscope for the presence of cancer cells.

There are several ways to get a biopsy. The method used is determined by the size of the breast or the abnormal area, where in the breast it is located, and the preferences of the doctor and the patient. Needle

Using a large needle, a tissue sample is taken from the breast during a core biopsy.

aspiration is the least invasive method. After numbing the skin with a local anesthetic, the doctor inserts a small needle that is attached to a syringe into the breast to collect and remove a sample of cells. If the area is difficult to palpate, the doctor may use ultrasound or mammography to help position the needle in the correct location. The procedure takes only a few minutes.

Similar to needle aspiration is a core biopsy. This procedure uses a slightly larger needle. As the needle is inserted, breast tissue cells fill the hollow interior of the needle. The needle is removed, and the sample is taken out of the needle for examination. In both procedures, several samples are taken to help ensure an accurate result.

Surgical Biopsy

Needle biopsies and core biopsies are quick, are relatively painless, and leave no scar, but because they take a very small sample of tissue, there is a risk that the cancer might be missed and lead to a false negative result. The doctor may recommend a surgical biopsy instead. Surgical biopsies are done in a hospital or out-patient surgery center, generally under local anesthesia, with some sedative medication given intravenously (through an IV). If the area is deep in the breast or if the patient prefers, they can be given a general anesthetic and sleep through the procedure. In a surgical biopsy, an incision, or cut, is made in the skin and the entire area of suspicion is removed, along with a small rim of tissue around it called a margin. The tissue is then sent to the lab for microscopic examination by a pathologist—a physician who specializes in diagnosing tissue cell abnormalities. In their report, the pathologist will describe the grade and stage of the cancer. Then, using special stains, they will examine the tissue for the presence of certain kinds of protein—hormone receptors and genetic markers—that can indicate what type of cancer is involved and what type of treatment is likely to work best.

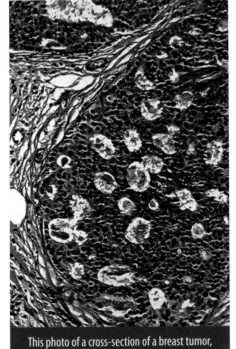

This photo of a cross-section of a breast tumor, taken under a microscope, was captured after the tumor was biopsied.

If the suspicious area is difficult to feel, the patient may go to the mammography center before the surgery and have a tiny wire inserted into the area, guided by mammography. This is called needle localization. Small barbs at the end of the wire hold the wire in place at the suspicious area. The surgeon uses the end of the wire as a guide to help make sure they remove tissue from the correct area. The wire is left in the tissue sample, which is sent back to the mammography center. There, the tissue itself is X-rayed to make sure the area of concern is included in the removed tissue.

Estrogen and Progesterone Receptors

If the biopsy is positive for cancer, one of the most important things it will be tested for is the presence of estrogen receptors or progesterone receptors in the cancer cells. Estrogen and progesterone are hormones that have very important functions in female sexual development and pregnancy. Estrogen also has an important role in healthy bone and heart function. The breasts, uterus, heart, and bones are all estrogen and progesterone target tissues. They have no effect on any tissues other than their target tissues.

Hormone receptors are specialized protein molecules on the surface of the cells of target organs, such as the breast, that allow the target organ to respond to the "messages" that the hormone brings. Of the two hormones, estrogen has the most impact on the development of breast cancer. A group of researchers from Cornell University in New York explained how estrogen receptors work:

> *Estrogen has a shape that allows it to fit into an estrogen receptor in the same way a key fits into a lock. The estrogen and the estrogen receptor bind to form a unit that enters the nucleus of the cell. The estrogen–receptor unit binds to specific sites on the cell's DNA, and this begins a series of events that turns on estrogen-responsive genes. These specialized genes instruct the cell to make proteins that carry out important activities. Some of these signaling proteins can tell the cell to divide.*[15]

Since estrogen stimulates cell division in its target organs, any mutation in the cell's DNA can become permanent as the cells divide and pass on the mutation to new cells. This is how estrogen helps some breast cancers grow.

About 80 percent of breast cancers have estrogen receptors on their cells and rely on the presence of estrogen to keep growing, and about 65 percent of these cancers also contain progesterone receptors. These tumors are said to be ER-positive or PR-positive. A tumor that is low in hormone receptors is called ER-negative or PR-negative. If a tumor's cells are ER-positive, doctors can prescribe a course of hormonal treatment that includes drugs called anti-estrogens, which interfere with the effect of estrogen on the cancer cells. The more receptors that are present, the more likely the tumor is to respond well to anti-estrogen hormone therapy.

HER2

About 25 percent of all breast cancers are referred to as HER2 positive. HER2 stands for "human epidermal growth factor receptor 2." It is a growth-promoting protein that is present on the outside of all normal breast cells. A HER2-positive cancer cell has an abnormally high number of copies of the HER2 gene. This causes too much HER2 protein to be on the surface of the cell. The cells then grow and divide abnormally fast. The HER2 status of a breast cancer is very important to know because HER2-positive breast cancer is particularly aggressive, and it may be more likely to recur in the future. One reason why HER2-positive breast cancers are so aggressive is because they are often associated with a protein called vascular endothelial growth factor (VEGF). VEGF stimulates angiogenesis—the growth of small blood vessels in the tumor that provide it with nutrients and oxygen and support its growth. Another reason they are dangerous tumors is that they are generally ER-negative, so they do not respond well to hormone therapy.

Controversy over Mammograms

For years, mammograms have been considered the most important tool in cancer detection, and women have been urged to get them regularly. Recently, however, they have come under fire for giving too many false positives. *Mother Jones* described a woman named Therese Taylor who was diagnosed with DCIS and had a mastectomy to treat it: "Taylor has come to realize that she lost her breast out of fear, not out of caution. She's learned that her mammogram was at least three times more likely to get her diagnosed and treated for a cancer that never would have harmed her than it was to save her life."[1] It can sometimes be difficult for doctors to tell which results on a mammogram are dangerous tumors and which are harmless abnormalities, which may lead to treatment recommendations that are too aggressive.

Some experts have recommended fewer mammograms to try to combat this problem, but other medical professionals oppose this move. According to Dr. Daniel Kopans, who has received funding from GE and Siemens—two companies that make mammogram equipment—underdiagnosis is a bigger problem than overdiagnosis: "Currently, we do not know which cancers will metastasize and kill and which, if any, can be left alone. Until we know the difference, we cannot just tell a woman to hold her breath, delay her mammogram, and wait."[2]

The debate about mammograms is ongoing, and the opinion of the medical community is divided. Some believe abnormalities that may not be dangerous should be treated less aggressively, while others believe early detection and treatment are necessary. Some suggest doctors should stop recommending mammograms completely and instead turn to more accurate screening methods—some of which are currently being developed. Ultimately, this medical decision is up to patients, and they should weigh the risks and benefits so they can make the best choice for themselves.

1. Christie Aschwanden, "What if Everything Your Doctors Told You About Breast Cancer Was Wrong?," *Mother Jones*, October 6, 2015. www.motherjones.com/politics/2015/10/faulty-research-behind-mammograms-breast-cancer/.

2. Daniel Kopans, "The Problem with the New Breast Cancer Screening Recommendations," *Forbes*, January 15, 2016. www.forbes.com/sites/matthewherper/2016/01/15/the-problem-with-the-new-breast-cancer-screening-recommendations/#31e8f7d3b4c4.

Monitoring Tests: Keeping an Eye on Breast Cancer

Monitoring tests are tests that are done after diagnosis and before, during, and after treatment. These tests help establish the overall health of the patient before starting treatment. They also assist doctors in evaluating the effectiveness of the treatment and allow the doctors to monitor the patient's health and strength during treatment. In addition, they are used to check for recurrence of the breast cancer and for metastasis to other parts of the body.

Among the first tests done are blood tests. A complete blood count, or CBC, shows the amounts of various kinds of blood cells present, such as white and red blood cells and platelets. White cells are part of the immune system and help fight off infections. Red cells are responsible for carrying oxygen to all the other cells in the body. Platelets have an important job in blood clotting. Cancer and its treatments can decrease the amounts of these important cells, so the cells are watched very closely. Another blood test frequently done during cancer treatment is blood chemistry. Blood chemistries give an indication of how well organs such as the liver, kidneys, and pancreas are functioning so any harmful effects of treatment on these organs can be managed. They also indicate if the patient is well-nourished enough.

Imaging Scans

Several different imaging studies are done for breast cancer patients to monitor the effectiveness of treatment and watch for recurrence and metastasis. The patient is likely to get a chest X-ray to see if the cancer has spread to the lungs and to make sure the heart and lungs are healthy enough for anesthesia before surgery and for the stresses of cancer treatment.

Several different types of scans may be given. A CT (computerized tomography) scan, also called a CAT (computerized axial tomography) scan, is an imaging technique using X-rays that gives a detailed picture of the inside of the body in cross-sectional views. During a CT scan, the patient lies on a narrow table that moves slowly through a donut-shaped machine that takes X-rays from several different angles. A computer puts the images together to give a series of pictures. CT scans may be used to evaluate large cancers that may have spread to the chest wall, or they may show metastases in other organs.

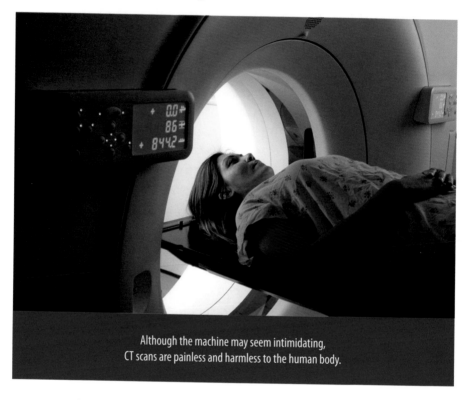

Although the machine may seem intimidating, CT scans are painless and harmless to the human body.

A PET (positron emission tomography) scan is another kind of scan that can detect areas of cancer. A PET scan actually gives a picture of the body's cells at work. Before the scan, the patient is given a sugar solution with a small amount of radioactive material added, called a tracer. Cancer cells tend to take up, or absorb, the radioactive sugar faster than noncancerous cells. The areas of high uptake show up on a computer screen and indicate where doctors need to look for possible cancer cells. PET scans help identify cancer that has spread to lymph nodes or other parts of the body, and they help assess the effectiveness of treatment.

A third type of scan is a bone scan, which shows whether breast cancer has spread to the bones. A bone scan may be done as soon as the diagnosis is made to establish a baseline image for comparison at a later time or to check for metastasis if the patient develops persistent pain in their bones and joints. During a bone scan, a radioactive tracer is injected into the bloodstream. The body is then scanned using a special type of camera. Areas of increased bone cell activity take up the material faster than areas of lower activity. These areas will show up as dark areas on the scan. Bone scans can also show other changes that are not cancer, such as arthritis. If the scan shows "hot spots" in the spine or joints, more testing may be needed to determine if they are caused by cancer or arthritis.

Thanks to improved methods of screening, many breast cancers are detected very early. Testing for hormone receptors and genetic markers further refine the diagnosis, which allows for more personalized treatment options for each patient and improves the chances for a positive outcome.

CHAPTER THREE

FIGHTING THE GOOD FIGHT

One of the reasons cancer is so feared is that it can be very difficult to treat or cure, even today. Unlike injuries or other diseases, which come from the outside world, cancer begins inside, turning the natural process of cell growth into a weapon against the body. Unfortunately, this means any attempt to attack a cancer is an attack on the person who has it, since it is their own body making them sick. Complicating the issue is the fact that even within the same cancerous tumor, there may be different types of cancer cells. Even though all the cells in a breast tumor begin with a breast tissue cell, as a cancer grows, the cells that make it up change, and new types of cancer cells are created within the same tumor mass. Each type has its own particular DNA "fingerprint." A treatment method that works on one type of cell may not work on another. For this reason, a combination of treatment methods may be used in a carefully planned sequence to get rid of as many different types of cancer cells as possible.

A diagnosis of breast cancer was once little better than a death sentence, but that is no longer the case. According to the website BreastCancer.org,

> In recent years, there's been an explosion of life-saving treatment advances against breast cancer, bringing new hope and excitement. Instead of only one or two options, today there's an overwhelming menu of treatment choices that fight the complex mix of cells in each individual cancer. The

decisions—surgery, then perhaps radiation, hormonal (anti-estrogen) therapy, and/or chemo-therapy—can feel overwhelming.[16]

Although treatment may be overwhelming, the survival rate for breast cancer is now about 90 percent, making it a battle people are much more likely to win.

Treatment Plans

Once the initial confusion and flurry of information after diagnosis has settled, it is time for the patient and their doctors to work together to decide on the most appropriate treatment options for the patient's particular case. "When you're in the midst of the diagnosis and staging process, and the tumor information is coming back in bits and pieces, at many different times, it is an extremely stressful time in your life," said Dr. Marisa Weiss, breast cancer expert and founder of BreastCancer.org. "But you will feel SO much better once you know what you're dealing with, when your treatment plan has been worked out, and you start your treatment. Only then does much of that dreadful uncertainty lift, and you finally feel that you are doing something to get rid of the problem."[17]

After diagnosis, it is important for a breast cancer patient to work closely with their doctors to create a treatment plan that is suited to their individual case.

Options for Treatment

The goal of breast cancer treatment is either to get rid of the cancer completely and achieve a total cure or to slow its growth, keep it from spreading, and help the person live for as long as possible. There are many options for treating breast cancer, and the methods chosen will depend on the specific type of cancer involved, the personal wishes of the patient, and the recommendation of the doctor. Treatment methods include different kinds of surgeries, chemotherapy, hormone therapies, and radiation therapy.

Surgery is often the first step in breast cancer treatment, depending on the nature of the cancer, its stage, and the personal needs of the patient. Many breast cancer patients have the option of having the entire breast removed, called a mastectomy, or they might choose breast-sparing surgery, called a lumpectomy, followed by radiation therapy and possibly chemotherapy. With either option, lymph nodes may or may not be removed as well.

Lumpectomy: Removing the Cancer

A lumpectomy is a surgical procedure in which only the cancerous area is removed along with a portion of normal tissue around it, called the tumor margin. It is similar to a surgical biopsy, except that it is for treatment rather than for diagnosis, so more tissue is removed to increase the likelihood of removing all the cancerous cells in the tissue. Like biopsies, lumpectomies may be done under local or general anesthesia. A lumpectomy takes about half an hour to complete.

Depending on the size of the tumor, the amount of tissue removed may be fairly small, or it may be as much as a quarter of the breast. If the suspicious area is small and difficult to feel, the patient may have needle localization first, just as it might be done before a biopsy, to help the surgeon locate the right area and assure they take enough of a margin around the area. The tissue removed is sent to the laboratory to be examined for the presence of cancer cells in the margins. If none are found, they are said to be clear. If one or more of the margins are not clear, another surgery will need to be performed so the surgeon can remove more tissue from that area.

When the procedure is done and the patient awakens from the anesthesia, they can go home. The doctor will prescribe pain medication to be taken at home if necessary. A lumpectomy is often followed by a course of radiation therapy. Chemotherapy may also be used as a follow-up treatment. These additional treatments are administered in an effort to achieve complete removal of all cancer cells in and around the affected area.

Mastectomy: Removing the Breast

A mastectomy is the removal of the entire breast. This procedure is recommended if the tumor is more than 5 cm in size, the breast is very small, clear tumor margins cannot be obtained, or the patient wants there to be no chance of the cancer coming back in the same breast. Depending on the type and stage of the cancer, a mastectomy may also be recommended for tumors smaller than 5 cm. For men, a mastectomy is much more common than a lumpectomy because they have less breast tissue to save. It is always done under general anesthesia and typically involves a hospital stay of two to three days. There are several different types of mastectomies, depending on how much tissue is actually removed.

A simple, or total, mastectomy involves removal of all the breast tissue, but no lymph nodes are removed from the axilla. A simple mastectomy is an option for patients who have the noninvasive DCIS, which is

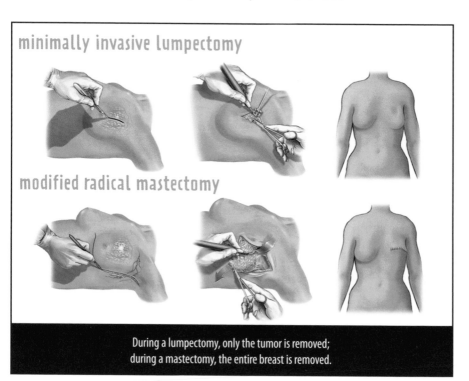

minimally invasive lumpectomy

modified radical mastectomy

During a lumpectomy, only the tumor is removed;
during a mastectomy, the entire breast is removed.

unlikely to spread. Patients who are already scheduled for breast cancer surgery may opt to have a simple mastectomy on the other side as well to avoid any chance of the cancer occurring in the other breast. This is called a prophylactic mastectomy.

A modified radical mastectomy involves removal of all the breast tissue as well as many of the lymph nodes in the armpit. A patient will need a modified radical mastectomy if it has already been determined that the cancer has spread to the nodes. The nodes are removed so they can be examined for the presence of cancer cells—a procedure called an axillary node dissection. Determining the number of nodes that are positive for cancer helps in staging the breast cancer and making decisions about further treatment methods. At the end of the procedure, just before the incision is closed, the surgeon will insert two to three drains—long narrow tubes that are attached to small collection bulbs that apply gentle suction to the inside of the incision. These help draw the fluids out of the incision into the bulb to keep them from collecting inside the incision, where they cause pain, infection, and delayed healing.

Another type of mastectomy is a skin-sparing mastectomy. In this mastectomy, a much smaller incision is made. Only the nipple, the areola, and the skin over the original biopsy site are removed, and the breast tissue is removed through this smaller incision. This is an option for patients who want to have their breast reconstructed by a plastic surgeon immediately after the breast is removed, during the same operation. It is not an option if the tumor is very close to the skin because there is too much of a chance that tumor cells will be left behind. It is also not an option for patients with IBC because radiation therapy is recommended after surgery, which can cause complications in a reconstructed breast. In the past, the relative survival rate for patients with IBC was so low that many doctors did not recommend reconstructive surgery, viewing it as unnecessary. Today, however, relative survival rates have improved to the point that a patient can request reconstruction surgery about two years after their mastectomy.

Sentinel Node Biopsy: Removing Lymph Nodes

During either a lumpectomy or a mastectomy, the patient may have an additional procedure called a sentinel node biopsy. The word "sentinel" means "to watch for" or "stand guard over." The idea behind a sentinel node biopsy is that, since cancer spreads outside the breast through the nodes, if the doctor can identify the first node it would be likely to spread to—the sentinel node—they can determine whether or not the cancer has spread.

When a patient who is scheduled for a sentinel node biopsy arrives at the hospital, they go to the nuclear medicine department, where procedures using radioactive substances are done. The area of the cancer is injected with a substance called a radioactive tracer. The tracer gives off very small amounts of radiation. After the injection, the patient goes on to the operating room, where the surgeon injects a blue dye into the same area. In the same way cancer cells spread into the lymph nodes, the radioactive tracer and the blue dye are taken up by the nodes.

After anesthesia is given and the patient is prepared for surgery, the surgeon makes a small incision near the armpit on the side of the cancer. They look for a node that has been stained blue from taking up the dye that was injected earlier. They also use a machine called a navigator, which can detect emissions of radioactive particles given off by the tracer. The navigator makes a series of clicking sounds that indicate how concentrated the radioactivity is. If the surgeon finds a node that is stained blue and also creates a lot of clicks on the navigator, it is considered to be a sentinel node. There are between one and five nodes that may be identified as sentinel nodes. The nodes are removed, sent to the lab, and examined microscopically for cancer cells.

If the sentinel nodes have no cancer cells, there is a 95 percent chance that the cancer has not spread out of the breast, and no further nodes need to be taken for staging purposes. If the sentinel node is positive for cancer cells, however, it means the cancer has already spread outside the breast. In this case, an axillary node dissection is necessary, even if the patient only had a lumpectomy.

Sentinel node biopsy is very valuable because it helps a patient avoid having to have an axillary node dissection unless it is absolutely necessary. This is important because the procedure can cause problems after surgery, such as numbness, weakness, or stiffness in the arm on the operative side. Another potential complication of axillary node dissection is called lymphedema, which occurs in about 10 to 12 percent of cases. When so many nodes are removed from the axilla, it changes the way lymph fluid normally moves through the arm and upper body. This can cause swelling and pain in the arm that can interfere with normal use of the arm.

Holistic Treatments

Many people feel that while doctors do a great job of treating disease, they sometimes may overlook or forget other needs of the patient—spiritual, mental, and emotional needs. Many patients and health care providers believe successful treatment of a disease requires attention to both the mind and the body. Treatment therapies that address these needs are called complementary, or holistic, medicine. They are seen as more gentle and natural than traditional methods involving surgeries, radiation, and drugs. They are typically used as a complement to standard treatment—along with, not instead of, traditional methods.

There are hundreds of kinds of complementary methods. A few examples of complementary medicine therapies include yoga, meditation and relaxation techniques, herbal supplements, hypnosis, massage, music therapy, and acupuncture. While complementary medicine has not been shown to treat breast cancer, it may, for many people, improve the quality of their lives while they are undergoing regular treatments. For example, yoga has been shown to reduce tiredness, ease anxiety and stress, and improve sleep. Acupuncture is known to help relieve hot flashes, tiredness, nausea, vomiting, and pain. Like other therapies, complementary therapies work better for some people than others, and deciding whether or not to use them is a personal choice.

Yoga may help breast cancer patients by easing stress and improving sleep while they are undergoing medical treatment.

Chemotherapy:
Using Drugs to Fight Cancer

After surgery, the first course of treatment is often chemotherapy, commonly referred to simply as "chemo." Chemotherapy is the use of drugs to treat cancer. Its purpose is to destroy any cancer cells that may remain after surgery. It may also be given before surgery to help shrink the size of the tumor so the patient may have the option of having a lumpectomy instead of a mastectomy. It is a systemic treatment, meaning the drugs travel through the bloodstream and can have their effect on cancer cells that may have already gone to other parts of the body. It also means the drugs may affect healthy cells as well. Chemotherapy drugs can be given through an IV, by injection, or by mouth.

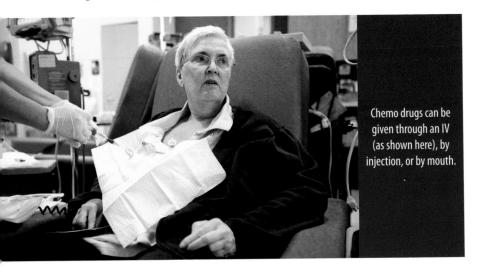

Chemo drugs can be given through an IV (as shown here), by injection, or by mouth.

Chemo is given in cycles. Each visit to the doctor or hospital for a dose of chemo drugs is one cycle. A cycle consists of a treatment period—which may take a day or two—followed by a recovery period, during which the patient rests and recovers from the side effects of the drugs, which can be unpleasant and cause weakness and fatigue. A course of chemo includes anywhere from four to eight cycles, given every two to three weeks depending on the nature of the tumor and the kind of drugs chosen for the treatment.

Chemotherapy drugs work by interfering with the growth and multiplication of rapidly dividing cells. This includes not only cancer cells, but also other areas of rapid cell growth, such as the blood, mouth, gastro-intestinal tract, and hair. Many of the drugs' side effects are expressed in these areas, leading to symptoms such as fatigue, diarrhea, constipation, mouth sores, hair loss, and nausea with vomiting. Healthy cells, however, are able to recover from the effects of the drugs and resume normal function once the course of chemo is over.

Not all breast cancer patients are candidates for chemo. Each individual case is unique, and what may be advised for one patient may not be advised for another. Factors doctors consider when deciding whether or not to prescribe chemo include the particular features of the cancer—its size and stage, hormone receptor status and HER2 status, and whether or not lymph nodes are involved. Because of the side effects, the patient's overall health status is considered. Chemo is never given to patients who have noninvasive in situ types of cancer because that type of cancer has almost no risk of spreading.

Hormones

Like chemotherapy, hormone therapy is a systemic treatment for breast cancer because it circulates throughout the body. It may be used after surgery to reduce the chances of the cancer coming back, or it may be used before surgery to decrease the size of the tumor. It can also be used to treat recurrent or metastatic cancer. It may be given at the same time as chemotherapy drugs, after a course of chemotherapy, or by itself.

The drugs used in hormone therapy come from sex hormones that are naturally present in both the male and female human body. They are used to treat cancers that grow in response to these hormones. They work by preventing the cancer cells from using the hormones they need to keep growing. They also work by preventing the body from making those hormones.

About two-thirds of all breast cancers are ER-positive, PR-positive, or both. These tumors can be treated by giving drugs that block the effect of estrogen or reduce the amount of estrogen made in the body. Hormone therapy does not work for tumors that are negative for hormone receptors.

The anti-estrogen drug Tamoxifen prevents estrogen from binding to the receptors in ER-positive cancer cells.

Several kinds of drugs are used in hormone therapy for breast cancer. Anti-estrogens such as Tamoxifen temporarily block estrogen receptors on the cancer cell, which prevents the estrogen from binding to the receptor. According to the American Cancer Society, taking Tamoxifen for 5 years after surgery decreases the chances of the cancer coming back by about 50 percent. Another drug called Faslodex not only blocks the receptors, it eliminates them altogether. It is used mainly in older patients whose cancer no longer responds to Tamoxifen. Aromatase inhibitors are another class of hormone therapy drugs. They work by blocking an enzyme called aromatase, which is responsible for estrogen production in the fat tissue of post-menopausal women. Other drugs work by shutting down production of estrogen in the ovaries of younger women.

Radiation

After chemotherapy treatments are complete, the breast cancer patient may also have a course of radiation therapy. Radiation therapy, or radiotherapy, is a cancer treatment that uses high-energy beams of radiation to destroy cancer cells. If chemotherapy is not going to be a part of the treatment plan, such as in noninvasive in situ cancers, radiation therapy may begin very soon after surgery.

Radiation damages cells by interfering with their DNA. This interferes with their ability to grow and duplicate themselves. Radiation therapy is often part of the treatment plan because even with clear margins, there is never an absolute guarantee that every last cancer cell is removed. Remaining cancer cells can continue to grow and form a new tumor. Radiation therapy helps lower the risk that cancer will recur after surgery. Many research studies have demonstrated that women with Stage 0 through Stage III cancers who have a lumpectomy or a mastectomy followed by radiation therapy have a lower chance of the cancer coming back than women who do not have radiation, even if the cancer is small. It can also be helpful for women with Stage IV cancer that has already spread.

Like chemo, radiation damages healthy cells as well as cancer cells, but healthy cells are better able to repair themselves after radiation treatment than cancer cells are. Dr. Marisa Weiss explained, "Cancer cell growth is unwieldy and uncontrolled—these cells just don't have their act together like normal cells do. When normal cells are damaged by radiation, they are like a big city with a fire and police department and trained emergency squads to come and 'put out the fire.' Damaged cancer cells are more like a disorganized mob with a bucket."[18]

External and Internal Radiation Therapy

There are two main ways to deliver radiation therapy—externally, from outside the body, and internally, with implanted devices that deliver radiation from the inside. External beam radiation therapy (EBRT) is the most common type of radiation therapy. It is generally started about a month after chemotherapy is completed, or about three to six weeks after surgery if chemotherapy is not given. It is delivered using a machine called a linear accelerator, which aims the radiation beam right at the area where the cancer was. This area is marked with small tattooed dots so the technicians know exactly where to aim the machine every time. A course of EBRT includes treatment sessions five days a week for five to seven weeks. Each treatment session lasts only a few minutes and is painless.

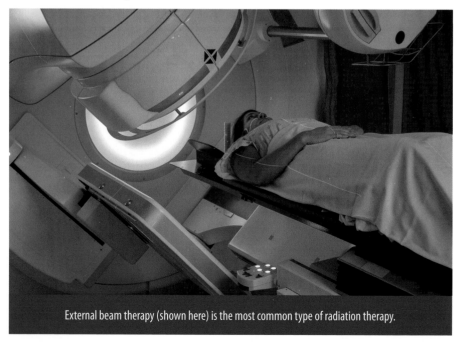

External beam therapy (shown here) is the most common type of radiation therapy.

Internal radiation is also referred to as partial breast radiation, or breast brachytherapy. The term "brachy" means "short distance," and brachytherapy administers radiation to a more focused area of the breast by inserting a catheter, or tube, directly into the breast, near the area of the cancer. It can be started immediately after surgery, or it can be given as a boost to a course of external beam radiation. The main advantage to brachytherapy is that the entire course of treatment lasts only one to two weeks instead of four to six. However, some recent research has suggested that although brachytherapy is more effective than no radiation at all, EBRT is better than brachytherapy at lowering the risk of needing a mastectomy later in life. Brachytherapy has also been shown to have a higher risk of infection and other post-operation complications than EBRT. Everyone's body is different, so patients should discuss the risks and benefits of brachytherapy versus EBRT with their doctor to decide if it is right for them.

Treatment for breast cancer can be extremely complex, confusing, and stressful, but few patients would make a decision not to do everything possible. Jeannette was 29 when she was diagnosed with both DCIS and inflammatory breast cancer. She underwent a bilateral mastectomy with axillary node dissection, chemo, radiation, and hormone therapy. "Cancer is a crap-shoot," she said. "There are so many factors to treatment and every person's biology reacts to treatment very differently. It's scary at first, but it is a fight that you begin as soon as you are diagnosed and never intend to quit. It's a commitment, sometimes a financial one, that takes a new-found strength because you MUST be your own advocate. Research, a knowledge-base, support, friends, etc., is essential to getting the treatment that's right for you."[19]

CHAPTER FOUR

SURVIVING BREAST CANCER

A diagnosis of breast cancer can be a devastating thing to hear. There is often an immediate reaction of fear. A newly diagnosed woman may worry about death; about the stress of treatment, surgery, and recovery; about the possibility of metastasis; and about the welfare of her family.

"I was devastated," said Kimalea Conrad, who was diagnosed in 2010. "I felt overwhelmed by fear. This disease was so dreaded and frightening. I thought it would change my life forever and I was discouraged. I felt my body had somehow betrayed me. I exercise and eat well, I am healthy. It seemed so unfair. I felt it was beyond my ability to cope."[20] The diagnosis can be just as disheartening for the woman's family as it is for her. In a 2010 study, researchers discovered that breast cancer patients' spouses saw the diagnosis as "unexpected, sudden, and emotionally overwhelming. They felt helpless to save themselves or their wives from what was happening. Every aspect of their daily lives and function was impacted, including job performance and social times with friends. They struggled to understand why such a thing would happen."[21]

The breast cancer patient must receive and process a great deal of information about the disease and its treatment. One of the first goals of the health care team is to reassure the patient that they have options, that their cancer can be treated, and that there will be support for them and their family along the way.

With the help of doctors and loved ones, several very important decisions must be made soon after diagnosis.

Surgical Decisions

One of the first decisions to be made involves surgery. For patients who are able to choose between a lumpectomy and a mastectomy, the decision can be complicated. Research has shown that a lumpectomy with radiation is often as effective as a mastectomy in terms of long-term survival from breast cancer, as long as there is only 1 cancer site, the tumor is less than 4 cm in size, and the tumor margins are clear. Additionally, recent research has found that age is an important factor; a study published in 2016 in the journal *European Society for Radiotherapy and Oncology* found that women under 45 "who opt for the more conservative surgery and radiation have a 13% higher local recurrence (such as a return of cancer in that breast or surrounding lymph nodes) over a 20-year period than those who have a mastectomy and no radiation."[22] This is because the disease progresses differently in older and younger patients, so although

It is important for newly diagnosed breast cancer patients to research their options for treatment, especially when considering surgery.

older women are more likely to develop breast cancer, younger women are more likely to see their cancer metastasize. Each treatment option has advantages and disadvantages, and each person's body is different, so all options should be discussed with a doctor.

The major advantage to a lumpectomy is that it preserves more of the natural size and shape of the breast. It generally does not require an overnight hospital stay, and recovery time is shorter and causes less discomfort than a mastectomy. One potential disadvantage is that as much as six weeks of radiation therapy is required after a lumpectomy to make sure any remaining cancer cells are eliminated. Also, depending on the type and stage of the cancer, there is some risk that the cancer will recur, or return, in the remaining breast tissue or that a new cancer will develop there. If that happens, the patient will have to go back to surgery for a mastectomy.

A mastectomy has the advantage of providing more peace of mind that the cancer will not come back on the same side because all the breast tissue has been removed. Disadvantages include that it is a more extensive surgery than a lumpectomy, involving more anesthesia, a longer recovery time, and more discomfort. To some, the loss of a breast may be seen as a disadvantage for cosmetic reasons, but reconstructive surgery and non-surgical prosthetics are often used to replace the breast if possible. Radiation may or may not be needed, depending on the nature of the cancer.

Some women who are very concerned about breast cancer occurring in the other breast may opt to have the healthy breast removed as well. Having cancer in one breast increases the chance that it will show up on the other side as well, especially if there is a strong family history of breast cancer. Women who do not have much of an emotional attachment to their breasts may decide to have both breasts removed, and so might women for whom surgical reconstruction of the breasts is an option. One woman explained her decision: "My decision to have a double mastectomy was guided by my age, family history and attitudes about my breasts. I'd gained weight and had actually become uncomfortable with my breasts, and all my life I'd had a history of tenderness in my breasts. So I felt I wasn't going to miss them very much."[23]

Surgical Reconstruction

Another important decision to be made is whether or not to have surgical reconstruction of the breast. Approximately 56 percent of women who have mastectomies go on to have surgical reconstruction. Reconstructive breast surgery is done by a plastic surgeon. It does not actually create a new breast, but it gives the woman the shape and feel of a new breast. Men may also choose to have their breasts reconstructed, but the process is different for them because the shape is much different than that of a woman's breast.

The simplest reconstruction method for women is the insertion of an artificial breast implant into a cavity created under the chest muscle. Breast implants come in many different shapes and sizes and are similar to

There are many different types of breast implants that may be used in reconstructive surgery.

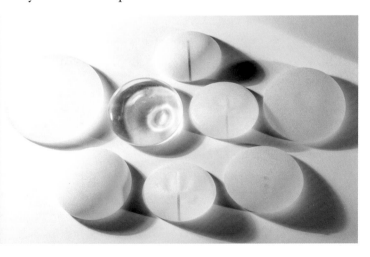

a small water balloon. They consist of an outer shell made of silicone. The shell is inserted into the cavity. The plastic surgeon then fills it with either saline (a diluted saltwater solution similar to natural tears) or silicone gel until it approximately matches the size of the remaining breast. The skin incision is then closed over the muscle. At a later time, after the patient has healed completely and the rest of her treatment is complete, she may opt to have the nipple and areola also reconstructed, to make the new breast look more natural.

Alternatively, she may choose to have them tattooed on. Tattoo artist Vinnie Myers has become famous for the realistic-looking nipples he tattoos onto reconstructed breasts. Myers explained why he has taken on this mission since 2001: "When you're looking at those breasts, all you see are the scars, and all you're reminded of is cancer … I want them to feel good when they're looking at themselves … So I tattoo the nipple and areola to look like a real nipple and areola, not like a brownish pink disc."[24] At one point it got so busy that he considered stopping, but the same day he made that decision, his sister called him to tell him she had breast cancer. He took it as a sign that he should continue his work and made nipple tattoos his full-time career. He charges between $400 and $800, but according to the Women's Health and Breast Cancer Right Act, which was signed into law in 1998, health insurance should cover the procedure. Myers's clients have said his tattoos boost their confidence by making them feel the way they did before they got cancer.

Tissue Flap Reconstruction and Oncoplastic Surgery

Tissue flap reconstructions are extensive surgeries that use skin, fat, and muscle from other areas of the patient's body to rebuild the breast. The advantage to this procedure is that the reconstructed breasts look and behave more like natural breasts, but the disadvantages include requiring more surgery, longer recovery time, and more scars. The most common methods are TRAM, DIEP, and latissimus dorsi flaps.

TRAM stands for "transverse rectus abdominis muscle." This muscle is located in the lower abdomen. To perform a TRAM flap, the surgeon removes a portion of the muscle, along with its fat and skin, from the lower abdomen. Its blood vessels are left in place so the flap keeps its blood supply, which is necessary for healing. A "tunnel" is created under the skin of the abdomen, and the tissue is passed through the tunnel and up into the space left by the mastectomy. The abdominal incision is closed and a new belly button is created. The tissue flap is shaped to closely match the other breast and sewn in place. A DIEP (deep inferior epigastric perforator) flap is also created with tissue from the abdomen, but it does not use muscle. In this procedure, skin and fat are cut completely from the abdomen and sewn onto the chest.

A latissimus dorsi flap, or "lat flap," is similar to a TRAM except that the muscle used is the latissimus dorsi, located along the back side of the upper chest. This flap may be used instead of a TRAM if the woman already has an implant but wants it to look more natural, if she has already had a TRAM on the other side, or if she has multiple abdominal scars from other surgeries. As with a TRAM, the tissue flap is passed under the skin, around to the front, and sewn into place. An implant can be placed behind the flap, if necessary, to help match the other side.

Some women are concerned about whether the size of their breasts will match after a surgery. This is a legitimate worry. Having breasts that are two very different sizes and shapes can affect a woman's confidence and also cause practical problems, such as making it difficult to find bras that fit. Surgeries that aim to preserve part of the breast, such as lumpectomies, do often cause this issue. To address this, some surgeons use a technique called oncoplastic surgery, which involves reshaping the breast during the lumpectomy or partial mastectomy. Sometimes this means a surgeon will operate on the other breast to make sure they match.

Controversy over Double Mastectomies

Recent trends have shown that more women—especially younger women—are choosing to get both breasts removed when cancer is found in one. Many medical experts discourage this because it is an unnecessary surgical procedure that increases the risk of infection and complications. However, according to the law, a woman has the right to make her own medical decisions, so

Going Flat

Although many women choose to replace their breasts through reconstructive surgery or prosthetics after a mastectomy, a growing number are choosing not to. As part of the global breast cancer support network promoted by social media, the "going flat" movement has gained traction over the past few years. From a medical standpoint, reconstructive surgery means more time under anesthesia and under the knife, more healing, and the possibility of more complications, such as blood clots and infection, that come with any surgical procedure. Because of these reasons, as well as concerns about health insurance and getting back to work quickly, about 44 percent of women choose not to get reconstruction. However, more and more are also foregoing prosthetics—fake, removable breasts—which can be heavy and uncomfortable.

Women refusing breast reconstruction and going without prosthetics is also part of a powerful social statement. Because breasts are traditionally associated with females and their sexual appeal in Western culture, a woman losing them and not wanting to have new ones calls into question society's definition of what is feminine and what is "sexy." Women are often reduced to sexual objects, told by the media that they are meant to be visually pleasing to men at all times. A woman without breasts, and without the illusion of breasts, goes directly against this idea in a surprisingly radical way, so much so that some men become angry at the thought of a woman going flat. In spite of this, more women are choosing to go flat and ignore social convention, reclaiming their bodies for themselves, for their own mental and physical well-being, and she may go against the advice of her doctors to get the surgery. Experts are uncertain why so many women are making this decision. It may be because they do not want to have to consider going through cancer again in the future, because they are concerned that their one reconstructed breast will not match their remaining natural breast, or for a combination of reasons.

Medical experts only encourage preventative double mastectomies in certain rare cases; for instance, if a woman carries a particular gene that increases her risk of breast cancer more than the average population. Researchers who have studied the double mastectomy trend have found that there is some misinformation surrounding the procedure, often reinforced by concerned friends and family. Mayo Clinic breast surgeon Judy C. Boughey explained that a double

not for anyone else. Some choose to get meaningful tattoos on their chests, while others do not. Since this movement is relatively new, some doctors may not understand it and may try to convince a woman to get reconstructive surgery. However, since going flat does not negatively impact a woman's health, they should not feel pressured to

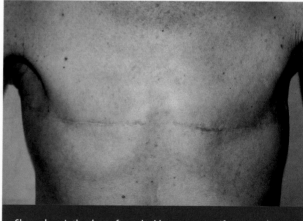

Shown here is the chest after a double mastectomy if a person chooses not to have breast reconstruction surgery.

follow a doctor's advice on this matter if they do not want to. Getting implants, going flat, and getting tattooed are personal decisions; women have the right to decide what will make them most happy and comfortable with themselves, and they are entitled to make their own medical decisions.

mastectomy does not improve a patient's chances for survival because although it prevents cancer from spreading in the other breast, it does not prevent it from spreading to other organs or bones. In her view, it has only negative consequences: Along with the increased risk of complications, "You can't breast-feed after having this done. There will be body image changes, sex life changes … But at the end of the day, the final decision is the woman's."[25]

Recovery

Recovering from breast cancer surgery is, in some ways, not unlike recovering from other types of surgery. Once they are home from the hospital, the patient will need to rest, take pain medication as needed, and watch the incision for signs of infection. They will need to rely on friends and family to help take care of daily needs at home.

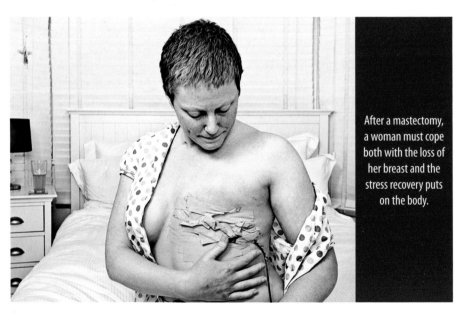

After a mastectomy, a woman must cope both with the loss of her breast and the stress recovery puts on the body.

If the patient has had an axillary node dissection along with the mastectomy, the doctor or nurse will teach them special exercises they can do to prevent stiffness and maintain mobility of their arm. These exercises must be done every day to keep the arm flexible and help prevent lymphedema—the swelling in the arm that can sometimes occur because of the removal of the lymph nodes in the axilla.

Another aspect of recovery from breast surgery is coping emotionally with the loss of the breast. Most men feel self-conscious about their scars at first, but it is less common for them to mourn the loss of their breasts than it is for women. Many women go through a period of grieving that has little to do with having cancer. Losing a breast can have serious implications for a woman's self-esteem and confidence. She may no longer feel attractive to her partner or spouse, or she may feel that part of her femininity has been taken away. It is very important for the woman to talk about these feelings with those who are close to her and also to remember that there is no one way to be beautiful, and no one way to be a woman, and breasts are not necessary for a fulfilling life.

Side Effects of Cancer Treatment

After the surgery is done and healing is complete, the treatment plan may include chemotherapy, radiation, hormone therapy, or a combination of several of these types of treatments. Although the treatments are designed to target cancer cells, they also affect healthy cells as well, so unpleasant side effects may occur. Side effects are undesired symptoms caused by the effects of treatment on other areas of the body. Most side effects are temporary and go away after treatment. Others may be chronic, which means they last for a longer time.

Of the different treatment therapies, chemotherapy has the most side effects. It is almost impossible to predict which side effects a patient will have because it depends on which drugs they are being given and on their body's particular response to the drugs. Some common temporary side effects of chemotherapy include fatigue, nausea and vomiting, hair loss, mouth sores, numbness or tingling in the hands or feet, and memory problems. Other side effects that are more serious and may cause long-term problems include blood changes, loss of bone density (osteoporosis), and damage to the heart. Fortunately, scientists have been able to develop effective methods to minimize side effects and manage them when they do occur.

As many as 70 to 80 percent of patients experience some amount of chemotherapy-induced nausea and vomiting (CINV). It generally lasts for just a few hours but can last for several days. It is important for the patient getting chemo to let their doctor know if they are experiencing CINV. Barbara Reville, a nursing director and cancer treatment specialist, said, "If you have problems with symptoms, they can be improved. You should call. I get very upset if someone says, 'I was throwing up,' but they never called. I hate that, because we could have helped them, if we had known."[26] The patient experiencing CINV can help control this side effect by eating several smaller, lighter meals instead of three big ones; avoiding foods high in fat; and not lying down for two to three hours after meals. Antinausea medications called antiemetics are very helpful for reducing or even preventing CINV.

Hair Loss

Another common side effect that may occur after a few cycles of chemo is hair loss. This can be a very difficult side effect to deal with emotionally, especially at first. Michele, a breast cancer survivor, said, "Some days I didn't want anyone to see me or even have my husband look at me."[27] Not all chemo drugs cause hair loss, and some women may just have thinning of their hair instead of total hair loss. Other

Cancer patients who lose their hair during chemo may choose to wear a head covering to protect their scalp.

women may lose the hair on all parts of their body, not just their head.

Hair almost always grows back after chemo is complete, but interestingly, it may grow back different: For example, straight hair may grow back curly, or thin hair may grow back thicker. It may even be a different color. "When you are waiting for your hair to grow," said Michele, "you spend a lot of time looking in the mirror, just waiting for a sign that you're going back to normal."[28] Women can try to help minimize the amount of hair loss by using gentle shampoos, cutting the hair short, using a low setting on the blow dryer, and avoiding chemical products such as perms or dyes. If a woman does lose all her hair, she can, if she chooses, help preserve her appearance and protect her scalp by wearing a hat, scarf, or wig. Many organizations, such as Pantene Beautiful Lengths, Wigs for Kids, and Locks of Love, turn donated hair into wigs they provide to cancer patients for free or at a greatly reduced cost.

Chemo's Effects on the Blood

Some chemo drugs can significantly lower the amounts of several types of blood cells. Neutropenia is the term for a low count of white blood cells, which are part of the immune system. Neutropenia can make a person more susceptible to infections, which may require hospitalization, and can weaken them to the point where further cancer treatment may be delayed. Anemia is a low count of red blood cells, which carry oxygen to all the cells of the body. Anemia can cause or worsen fatigue and weakness. A lower than normal number of platelets in the blood, which are needed for proper clotting, is called thrombocytopenia. Low platelets can cause bruising or prolonged bleeding if the patient gets a cut. Most of these problems can be treated with medications or, if necessary, a transfusion of blood or platelets.

Effects on Fertility

Premenopausal women receiving hormonal therapy to stop the action of estrogen may experience symptoms similar to menopause, such as irregular or absent menstrual periods, hot flashes, mood swings, and loss of bone strength. Younger woman on chemo may worry about how it will affect their fertility—the ability to have children in the future. The younger the woman is, the more likely it is that her ovaries will resume normal function after chemo is completed and she will be able to get pregnant if she wants. About half of the patients under the age of 35 resume regular menstrual cycles and are fertile after treatment. Certain drugs, especially those called alkylators, and higher doses of other chemo drugs are more likely to cause infertility. Other drugs, such as methotrexate, have little effect on fertility.

Another concern is the effect of chemo drugs on an unborn child if the woman is pregnant or if she becomes pregnant during treatment. Chemo drugs can cause genetic damage to immature eggs while they are still in the ovaries. They may also cause birth defects in the unborn child as it develops. The drug methotrexate, for example, is not likely to hinder fertility but may increase the risk for spinal cord defects in the unborn baby. Most doctors encourage women to wait at least six months after chemo is completed before trying to get pregnant.

After treatment, about 50 percent of cancer patients under 35 regain their fertility and are able to have children.

Radiation Side Effects

The side effects of radiation are generally not as severe as those from chemotherapy, and not every patient will experience them. Like chemo side effects, they are often temporary and should go away when treatment is done. Also, as with chemo, the patient getting radiation therapy should make sure their doctor knows about any side effects they may experience so they can decide together on the best way to manage the side effects.

The most common side effect is skin irritation, similar to a sunburn, caused by the radiation. The skin may become reddened, sensitive, dry, or flaky. It may even blister or peel. It may be worse in the armpit or under the breast, where there is more skin friction. It may also be worse in fair-skinned patients or women with large breasts. Skin irritation can be helped by staying out of the sun, avoiding very hot or very cold water, wearing loose clothing, and using a soothing lotion. Radiation may cause some tenderness or swelling in the breast or chest wall around the treated area. It may also worsen fatigue for some patients. In addition, it can also cause certain heart or lung problems, such as coughing, difficulty breathing, rapid or irregular heartbeat, and swelling in the legs. Like chemo, it may also lower white blood cell counts.

Supporting a Loved One

There are many sources of support for breast cancer patients: community support groups, religious organizations, and networks of friends, family, and coworkers. During a time of such high stress, it is important to have help with daily needs such as meals, errands, housework, and child care when energy and morale are low. Marilyn, a breast cancer patient, said, "You have to open up and let other people help you. The way I was able to do it was to realize that it helps them to help you. So you're actually doing them a favor by letting them help you!"[29]

It can be very helpful for a breast cancer patient to be able to talk with other patients who have gone through the same experiences and challenges and have met them successfully. Most communities provide contact information to groups of other patients who have or had breast cancer and can help in this way. For some patients, spending some time talking with a therapist or church leader can help relieve some of the emotional burden and help them learn effective ways to cope with anxiety or depression.

Support from loved ones is incredibly important during this stressful time, but often, loved ones are unsure how to help. This uncertainty may stop them from reaching out, but this is the time when a person with cancer needs their friends and family most of all. Not reaching out puts an extra burden on someone who is already dealing with a lot of stress; they may feel abandoned or feel as if they are bothering others with requests for help. Sometimes, all that is needed is a listening ear and a shoulder to cry on. Other times, the person may need a ride somewhere, a healthy meal, or some other type of help. Loved ones should not act angry or offended if their offers of help are turned down, as the person with cancer is not required to accept every offer of help, especially if they do not need or want what is being offered at the time.

Some patients and survivors find support groups helpful.

Sometimes, loved ones mean well but say things that are offensive or upsetting to a person with breast cancer. Some of these include:

- "I know you'll be fine."
- "I'm so worried about you!"
- "At least it's not [some other disease or type of cancer]."
- "My mom had that and she used [specific treatment/diet/herbal remedy/etc.]. You should try it."
- "Just let me know what you need."
- "I know how you feel."

- "Why don't you wear a wig?"
- "Does it feel weird having just one breast?"
- "What do you think caused it?"
- "You don't look sick."
- "Will the cancer come back?"
- "Keep me updated on your treatment."

Many of these comments sound supportive, but in reality, they may make a person with cancer feel worse. For instance, someone telling someone how worried and upset they are may make the patient feel as though they need to comfort their friend, when it should be the other way around. Giving people unwanted advice on their medical treatment is often considered rude and unwelcome. Telling the patient to communicate their needs puts a burden on them because often they do not know what they need ahead of time; it is better to ask if the patient needs something specific—for example, "Do you want me to make you some food?" Asking too many

Support in the Struggle: Reach to Recovery

One of the oldest support organizations for women with breast cancer is Reach to Recovery. It was founded in 1952 by Terese Lasser of New York City. During her hospital stay for breast cancer, she felt totally alone with her questions and fears. She took it upon herself to get the answers to her questions and decided that no woman should have to face breast cancer alone. She began to visit other women who were struggling with cancer and found that having the support of another person with similar experiences was mutually beneficial. Over time, the network grew, and in 1969, Reach to Recovery joined with the American Cancer Society and became a nationwide organization.

Reach to Recovery provides highly trained volunteers who are breast cancer survivors themselves. The volunteers are available to anyone who has been newly diagnosed with breast cancer, is undergoing treatment, or has completed treatment and is dealing with side effects or metastasis. They provide emotional support and current information to patients through personal attention on the phone, at home, or anywhere the patient wants to meet. Today, with financial support from several large companies and foundations, Reach to Recovery is available to breast cancer patients and their families in almost every community in the United States.

questions about how the treatment is progressing or telling the person repeatedly they will beat the cancer may make the patient feel anxious, especially if it does not appear that the treatment is working well.

The best ways to support a loved one with breast cancer are to listen without passing judgement or giving advice, be available to help when needed, celebrate small victories, stay patient, and keep their spirits up by doing things they enjoy.

Recurrence

After surgery is done and treatment is completed, the fight is not always over. Most cancer survivors fear the cancer may come back, either in the same place or in another part of the body. Additionally, the experience of going through cancer treatment often changes the way a person feels about life. Psychiatric nurse Shari Baron runs support groups for women with breast cancer. "In my groups," she said, "we talk about 'BC' and 'AC'—Before Cancer and After Cancer. You can never go back to Before Cancer. You wonder: Will the cancer come back? The fear does lessen over time. But it's never gone completely."[30]

If breast cancer comes back in the same breast or if it returns very close to the original place, it is called a local recurrence. Two-thirds of breast cancers that come back are local recurrences. Recurrences may be found by mammography, physical examination, or both. There may be extra tests such as an ultrasound or an imaging study, especially if the woman had reconstruction with an implant, to help determine if the new mass is really a recurrence of cancer, something harmless, such as scar tissue, or an infection. If cancer returns in a different part of the breast or in the other breast, it is probably not a recurrence of the same cancer but a new cancer altogether. It is even possible for a new cancer to appear after a mastectomy in the few normal breast tissue cells that may remain after surgery.

Breast cancer that comes back in the lymph nodes in the axilla, the neck, near the chest wall, or under the collarbone is called a regional recurrence. The woman may notice enlarged, round lumps in her armpit or in her neck, or they may be seen on a follow-up mammogram. When this happens, it is likely the cancer is back in the breast or chest wall as well as the nodes. A surgical biopsy is done to check for cancer cells in the enlarged nodes.

Metastatic breast cancer is cancer that has traveled to some other part of the body, most commonly the bones, lungs, brain, or liver. It is generally found when the person develops symptoms in the area to which it has spread. For example, if it spreads to the bones, they may feel persistent back or joint pain. In the brain, there may be headaches, blurred vision, confusion, or loss of balance. A spread to the lungs may cause a persistent cough, shortness of breath, or pain in the chest. Symptoms of cancer that has spread to the liver may include abdominal pain, a yellowish color in the skin and eyes called jaundice, abnormal blood tests, or loss of appetite. If these symptoms develop, the doctor will order more tests to determine their cause. These may include chest X-rays or ultrasounds; scans such as CT scans, PET scans, or bone scans; or possibly a biopsy of the area in question.

Once metastasis is confirmed, a course of treatment must be developed involving more chemo, radiation, surgery, or newer experimental therapies. This is something each patient must consider thoughtfully and discuss thoroughly with their doctor and family so the patient's needs and wishes are met. Family issues, financial matters, and personal feelings and attitudes all come into play when considering how metastatic disease is going to be managed. Some patients want aggressive treatment, despite the side effects it may cause. Others choose not to treat their disease aggressively because they do not want to spend their days suffering from side effects. They may choose treatments that address only the symptoms of the disease, such as pain medications, steroids to reduce swelling, draining excess fluid from around the lungs to ease breathing, or medications to strengthen bones weakened by the cancer.

A Shifted Perspective

Fighting breast cancer is an enormous struggle, and those who survive it often approach life with a different outlook. Robyn was 36 when she was diagnosed with Stage III breast cancer. "Cancer has made me stronger in so many ways," she said. "I have learned to not sweat the small stuff and try to always look at the big picture. It has made me realize how amazing my family and friends can be. The biggest life lesson that I have learned is to appreciate what you do have, take the time to smell the roses."[31]

Shown here is a woman who chose not to have breast reconstruction surgery following a double mastectomy. It is often important for patients to feel like they have options and choices during treatment and recovery.

New treatment methods for recurrent and metastatic breast cancer have greatly improved survival, and research continues at a fast pace. Living with breast cancer is not nearly as difficult as it once was, thanks to much improved knowledge, treatment methods, techniques for managing side effects, and greatly expanded sources of help and support.

CHAPTER FIVE

FOR THE FUTURE

Over the past four decades, few diseases have been given as much attention as breast cancer. Because of this explosion in awareness and knowledge, major advances have taken place in the areas of screening, diagnosing, treating, managing, and even preventing breast cancer. Every year, thousands of charities donate money to breast cancer research to better the chances of survival for future patients and to hopefully find an ultimate cure. With every discovery and invention, more women are saved or have their lives improved. Right now, around the world, a number of research projects are underway in an effort to improve the ways breast cancer is treated and prevented.

Testing New Treatments

When a new treatment or procedure is first developed, it is tested in a laboratory on tissue samples or animals. These early tests are called preclinical trials. If the preclinical trials suggest the new treatment might be safe and effective in people, clinical trials begin. Clinical trials are research projects that study how well the new treatment works on living human beings who have the disease or condition on which the treatment is designed to work. They are important because they establish whether or not the treatment is safe and effective in humans.

It takes a long time for a drug or other treatment method to move from preclinical to clinical trials, and

It may take many years for a new treatment to make it through trials because researchers must be sure it is safe for human consumption.

many do not ever get that far. The American Cancer Society estimates that only 1 out of 1,000 new medicines makes it to clinical trials. Drugs that are currently used in breast cancer treatment have all been through years of preclinical trials followed by several more years of clinical trials. It takes many years to complete a clinical trial because researchers need to test the treatment in as many human volunteers as possible to get the most accurate information. They also need to study how the drug works over time so they can get a clear picture of any long-term side effects the drug or treatment may have.

Clinical trials are generally done in four phases. Each phase builds upon the information learned during the previous phase. In Phase I trials, the goal is to determine whether the treatment is safe for people. Since safety is unknown at this point, the test group is small, generally fewer than 50 people. Phase II focuses more on the most effective dose of the treatment, based on the information learned in Phase I. The study group is larger in Phase II—about 100 people. In Phase III, the new treatment is compared to treatments that already exist to see if it is any better. Phase III may involve thousands of people and may collect data contributed by hospitals and other treatment centers all over the world. When Phase III is complete, it is time for the U.S. Food and Drug Administration (FDA) to consider its approval for the treatment. After FDA approval, the treatment may or may not enter a Phase IV. This phase looks at possible long-term effects of the treatment that may not show up during earlier phases. It also studies the possibility of other unexpected benefits the treatment may reveal over time.

Thousands of clinical trials are underway all over the world to find new and better ways to screen for, diagnose, treat, and manage breast cancer. The hope of these trials is to minimize the risk of getting breast

Vaccination Against Breast Cancer

A vaccine is a drug that stimulates the body's immune system to recognize and attack invading disease organisms. Vaccines have been used for a long time to prevent illnesses such as measles, polio, and tetanus. Researchers have been working for decades to develop a vaccine that would fight cancer cells and help prevent cancer from recurring after treatment—a technique called immunotherapy. Developing an effective cancer vaccine is difficult because vaccines are generally made from foreign invaders such as bacteria or viruses, but it is much more difficult to create a vaccine that will attack the body's own cells, especially without harming healthy ones. Another stumbling block is that cancerous tumors contain many different types of cancer cells, and a vaccine would be limited to attacking only the types it could recognize.

In March 2017, *Breast Cancer News* announced that the U.S. Department of Defense would give researchers at the Mayo Clinic $3.7 million to conduct a Phase II trial of a vaccine to treat women with DCIS. About 45 women are enrolled in the trial, which was proposed to begin in 2017. It was announced that participants would receive the vaccine, called TPIV 110, six weeks before having surgery to remove the tumor. TPIV 110 targets HER2. Since only some breast cancer cells have higher than normal levels of this protein, the vaccine can target some, but not all, types of breast cancer. The leaders of the TPIV 110 trial hope the vaccine can eventually be used to eliminate certain breast cancers without surgery or radiation. Other types of breast cancer vaccines are also currently being tested.

cancer and to improve the survival from this disease. Other types of research studies, such as demographic studies that look at certain populations of people and their risk of disease, are also being conducted in an effort to learn as much as possible about breast cancer.

Learning the Risk Factors

One very important step in conquering breast cancer is to learn more about who is at risk and which factors increase the risk so doctors and their patients can become better educated about how they can reduce their risk. Many research studies are finding that certain factors seem to increase risk, such as smoking, alcohol consumption, obesity, and certain environmental chemicals. Other studies are discovering what may decrease risk, such as regular physical exercise, vitamin D, anti-inflammatory drugs such as aspirin, and breastfeeding. Still others study substances such as caffeine, birth control pills, and fertility drugs to determine what effect, if any, these substances have on breast cancer risk.

One of the most active areas of breast cancer research involves how lifestyle choices affect risk. This is important because lifestyle choices are things people can control. Smoking is one lifestyle choice that has been linked to many different health problems, including breast cancer. Cigarette smoke contains dozens of different chemicals, most of which are very toxic to the human body and are capable of causing the genetic mutations that lead to the beginning of cancer growth.

One group of researchers at the University of Toronto conducted what is called a meta-analysis—they reviewed several studies that all focused on smoking and breast cancer. Dr. Neil Collishaw, the chairman of the group, said, "Until recently, evidence about the link between breast cancer and tobacco smoke …

was inconclusive. But the panel's careful analysis of all available evidence, particularly recent evidence, led us to believe that there is persuasive evidence of risk."[32] The group found that the incidence of breast cancer is 20 percent higher in premenopausal women who smoke, especially when they start young, when their breast tissue is not fully developed. Non-smokers are also at increased risk even if they are only exposed to secondhand smoke. A 2008 study from Harvard University in Boston, Massachusetts, concluded that nicotine, even from secondhand smoke, can trigger both normal and cancerous breast tissue cells to grow and migrate—both within the breast and outside the breast. This study showed that nicotine exposure also increases the risk of developing a second breast cancer sometime in the future.

Another lifestyle factor that appears to have an impact on breast cancer risk is obesity. In 2001, researchers concluded that obesity and physical inactivity are related to an increased risk of several kinds of cancer, including breast cancer. Overweight, postmenopausal women have almost twice the risk of getting breast cancer as women of normal weight, and their risk of dying from breast cancer is also higher. Weight may also affect the type of breast cancer a woman develops. The very aggressive IBC is much more common in overweight women. "The more obese a patient is, the more aggressive the disease," said cancer expert Dr. Massimo Cristofanilli. "We are learning that the fat tissue may increase inflammation that leads to more aggressive disease."[33]

Several studies have looked at the impact of healthy diet or exercise in breast cancer survivors, as well as their ability to lower the risk of contracting breast cancer at all. A 2007 study looked at the effects on survival time of both diet and exercise together. "It looks like if you get your physical activity going and get your fruits and vegetables in [five or more servings], you can reduce your risk (of dying) significantly," said Dr. John Pierce, one of the researchers. The survival benefit was true even for obese women who adopted the healthier lifestyle. "Doing each alone didn't do it," Dr. Pierce said. "There was no benefit from each alone, but there was a benefit from both together."[34]

Eating healthy and exercising have been proven to reduce the risk of developing breast cancer as well as the chances of recurrence.

Studies such as these, as well as the Million Women Study—which, in 2001, demonstrated the significantly increased risk associated with alcohol consumption—highlight the importance of choosing a healthy lifestyle to aid in the prevention of breast cancer or increase survival in women who develop the disease. Additionally, according to the Centers for Disease Control and Prevention (CDC), some types of birth control pills can increase the risk. Women who are taking birth control should discuss these risks with their doctor. These are risk factors that can be controlled, and making the right choices can make a big difference.

Controlling certain risk factors is important

because, unfortunately, other risk factors cannot be controlled. These include:

- being a woman
- having dense breasts
- getting older
- having a family history of breast cancer
- certain genetic mutations

Some current research focuses on using medications to affect the risk factors that cannot be otherwise controlled. This includes hormone therapy as well as studying dietary supplements and the side effects of medications prescribed for other ailments. For instance, taking nonsteroidal anti-inflammatory drugs (NSAIDs) such as ibuprofen, which is typically used to treat minor pain such as headaches and muscle aches, may have the unintended side effect of lowering breast cancer risk. If researchers can prove this, they may be able to recommend these medications to women with a high genetic risk. However, this research is still ongoing, and it may be many years before scientists can prove that these medications work this way.

Improved Screening

Research is underway to develop new and better methods of screening women for breast cancer. One experimental method being studied is molecular breast imaging (MBI), also called scintimammography. MBI uses a slightly radioactive tracer, which is injected into the bloodstream. The tracer attaches to breast cancer cells and can be seen with a special camera. MBI appears to be beneficial for women with dense breast tissue that may hide a possible cancer on a regular mammogram. It is also much less expensive than an MRI. Not only is MBI better able to detect breast cancers, it also yields fewer false positives than a mammogram, which decreases the number of unnecessary breast biopsies.

Another new screening test is called digital tomosynthesis. Digital tomosynthesis uses X-rays, like a digital mammogram, but it creates a three-dimensional (3D) view of the breast, rather than the two-dimensional image created by a mammogram. It takes images of the breast from at least 11 different angles, instead of the 2 that mammograms take. The test does not require uncomfortable compression of the breast, and it takes only seconds to complete. The images are sent to a computer for conversion into a 3D image. Researchers have proven that digital tomosynthesis can help detect cancers in dense breast tissue, and they hope the improved comfort will lead more women to have regular screenings performed. It has been FDA approved, but it is not yet common and can only be found at a limited number of hospitals.

Genetic Discoveries

The field of genetics has provided an entirely new way of approaching breast cancer and its treatment. With the discovery of the BRCA1 and BRCA2 gene mutations, the HER2 gene, and others, the door was opened to new ways to fight the disease. Discoveries in genetics continue to help doctors refine treatment plans to make them less uncomfortable, more effective, and more individualized for each patient.

In 2016, five new genes were discovered to be associated with breast cancer. After analyzing 560 patients' genetic histories, researchers found that these 5 genes are likely to mutate and influence the growth of tumors. With these new genes identified, it became apparent that breast cancer genomes—the entire genetic code of the cancer—are as individual as the people they come from, making it easier to create a highly targeted treatment plan. "In the future," said Dr. Serena Nik-Zainal from the Wellcome Trust Sanger Institute, who led the study, "we'd like to be able to profile individual cancer genomes so that we can identify the treatment most likely to be successful for a woman or man diagnosed with breast cancer. It is a step closer to personalised healthcare for cancer."[35]

Genetic and Genomic Testing on Cancer Cells

Over the past 15 years, genetic testing done on the cancer tissue itself has become more popular. These tests help determine the genetic makeup of cancer cells, which can tell doctors about how the cancer will behave and what treatment plan will be the most effective. The Spot-Light HER2 CISH test was approved for use in 2008. It determines whether a breast tumor is HER2 positive or negative. It is important to know this because HER2-positive cancers are especially aggressive and fast-growing. They also tend to be hormone receptor-negative, so they will not respond well to hormone therapy. They do, however, respond to a drug called Herceptin, which blocks the message to grow and divide that the HER2 protein sends to the cell. The test uses a special stain, which is applied to the tumor tissue and colors the HER2 genes. This shows how many copies of the gene there are in the tumor cells. The more copies of the gene there are, the more HER2 protein will be present on the surface of the cell.

Another test done on cancer tissue is called the Oncotype DX test. This test is done on breast tumors that are early stage, ER-positive, and lymph node negative—cancers that will respond to hormone therapy and that have not spread outside the breast. These cancers have a very low risk of recurring, but a small number of them do still recur after treatment. This test helps determine if the patient's cancer is one that has a higher than normal risk of recurrence. It also helps a doctor decide whether or not a patient needs chemotherapy, as well as hormone therapy, to reduce the risk of recurrence.

The Oncotype DX is a genomic test, which means that unlike a genetic test, which looks for inherited genetic mutations, it examines a group of 21 different genes and their activity in the cancer cell. It gives the tumor its own genetic "personality" in the form of a recurrence score. A score of less than 18 indicates a low risk of recurrence, from 18 to 31 is considered intermediate, and a score more than 31 indicates a high risk. When combined with other information about the tumor, doctors and their patients can make a more informed decision about whether the benefits of chemotherapy would outweigh the side effects.

Up and coming in the United States is the MammaPrint test. Although it has been around since 2005, it is most popular in Europe and is only beginning to get widespread recognition in the United States. Like the Oncotype DX test, it is used on early-stage cancers to determine the likelihood that they will recur up to 10 years after diagnosis. Unlike the Oncotype DX, however, it can be used on invasive cancers that have spread to up to three lymph nodes as well as on ER-negative cancers. Its move into the spotlight was triggered by researchers who attended the annual meeting of the American Association for Cancer Research in 2016. They presented the

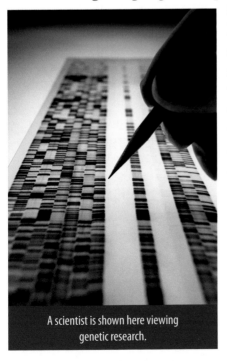

A scientist is shown here viewing genetic research.

findings of the MINDACT trial, a study based in Europe examining the MammaPrint's ability to predict whether an early-stage cancer will come back. According to *Forbes* magazine, "The main finding, so far, is that early-stage breast cancer patients with low … MammaPrint risk results do well regardless of whether or not they receive chemotherapy. With a median follow-up of 5 years, their metastasis-free survival exceeds 94%."[36] MINDACT is a relatively new study, so it may not hold up in the long-term. However, while some still have reservations about MammaPrint, many have been convinced that it would be a useful tool in treating and monitoring breast cancer if it were more widely accepted.

Cancer Stem Cell Research

The traditional approach to treating cancer has been to kill as many cells in the tumor as possible. New research being done in several centers around the world is now suggesting this may not be as effective in preventing recurrences of cancer because the wrong cells are being targeted. The research has identified certain kinds of cancer cells, called cancer stem cells, that may be responsible for creating all the other cancer cells in a tumor and for creating new cancers.

Stem cells are immature cells that have not yet differentiated into any particular kind of cell. Cancer stem cells not only reproduce themselves, they can also become other types of cancer cells within the same tumor. Research at the University of Michigan showed that only 1 to 3 percent of tumor cells are stem cells, and as few as 100 to 200 of these stem cells, injected into mice, were capable of starting new tumors. The research has also shown that cancer stem cells are particularly difficult to kill, which may explain why some cancers recur even after aggressive treatment. The research suggests that drugs need to be developed that will target cancer stem cells and eliminate them, thereby eliminating their opportunity to create new cancers.

Biological Therapies

Discovering more about the role of genetics in breast cancer has led to the development of more advanced methods of therapy called targeted, or biological, therapies. Whenever a unique characteristic of a cancer is identified, such as a gene, a protein, or a unique cellular process, drugs can be developed to treat that characteristic as a target and interfere with that particular characteristic. They can tell a particular gene or protein what to do to stop cancer growth. Targeted therapies specifically target only cancer cells, their genes, and the proteins they make. They do not harm normal, healthy cells, so their side effects tend to be milder than traditional chemotherapy. At this time, targeted therapies are being used along with traditional chemotherapies.

One of the first targeted therapies to be FDA approved was Herceptin, which was first approved for use in breast cancer treatment in 1998. Since then, trials have been conducted to evaluate its effectiveness when used along with other treatments, as well as to establish the most beneficial length of time for treatment. Herceptin is a kind of drug called a monoclonal antibody—a synthetic, or man-made, version of an immune system protein. Herceptin specifically targets HER2-positive cancers, attaching itself to the HER2 protein and interfering with its growth signals to the cell. It may also help stimulate the immune system and help it attack cancer cells. Another kind of targeted therapy works by interfering with angiogenesis—the growth of new blood vessels that supply the tumor cells.

Herceptin powder for

In 1998, Herceptin became the first FDA-approved targeted therapy for breast cancer.

The newest class of targeted therapy drugs is the

poly ADP-ribose polymerase (PARP) inhibitors. PARP is a protein that repairs damage in the DNA of cancer cells. If a cancer cell's DNA has been damaged by radiation or chemo, for example, the PARP protein can fix it, making the treatment less effective. PARP inhibitors interfere with PARP's ability to repair damaged DNA. They can be effective in patients with the BRCA1 and BRCA2 mutations, even to the point of preventing breast cancer from ever starting in women who have inherited these mutations. They can also be effective for treating the very difficult triple-negative form of breast cancer, and they are proving useful for other types of cancer, such as ovarian cancer. They do not affect healthy cells at all, only cancer cells.

Research is showing that attacking breast cancer at the level of its DNA may be the core of breast cancer treatment in the future. Promising new targeted therapies are being developed and perfected that will be highly effective and very selective, improving survival and minimizing side effects.

Not a Struggle Forever

Although people all over the world are struggling with breast cancer, it is hardly the threat it used to be. In her book, *The New Generation Breast Cancer Book*, Dr. Elisa Port pointed out that "we are using less invasive surgery and treatments while still achieving better outcomes, and offering more options for reconstruction than ever before,"[37] and her optimism is justified. While fear is a natural reaction to any serious health problem, it no longer has to set the tone for someone's entire outlook on breast cancer. With new technology and treatments coming out every year, the shadow looming over a breast cancer diagnosis is being removed. Someday, medical experts may have enough tools to make beating breast cancer a possibility for every patient.

Introduction: Struggling and Surviving Together

1. Samantha Stephenson, "Samantha Stephenson—Breast Cancer Survivor," Cancer Treatment Centers of America, 2017. www.cancercenter.com/community/survivors/samantha-stephenson/.

2. Quoted in Cordelia S. Bland, "The Halsted Mastectomy: Present Illness and Past History," *Western Journal of Medicine*, June 1981, p. 549.

3. Quoted in Greg Botelho, "Breast Cancer: The Path Traveled and the Road Ahead," CNN, October 11, 2005. www.cnn.com/2005/HEALTH/02/22/breast.cancer/index.html.

4. Quoted in Deborah Axelrod, Rosie O'Donnell, and Tracy Chutorian Semler, *Bosom Buddies: Lessons and Laughter on Breast Cancer*. New York, NY: Warner Books, 1999, p. 1.

5. Quoted in Axelrod, O'Donnell, and Semler, *Bosom Buddies*, p. 1.

6. Quoted in Botelho, "Breast Cancer," CNN.

7. Quoted in Botelho, "Breast Cancer," CNN.

Chapter One: Breast Cancer 101

8. Rosalind Benedet, NP, and Mark C. Rounsaville, MD, *Understanding Lumpectomy—A Treatment Guide for Breast Cancer*. Omaha, NE: Addicus Books, 2004, p. 4.

9. Yashar Hirshaut, MD, and Peter I. Pressman, MD, *Breast Cancer, The Complete Guide*, 5th ed. New York, NY: Bantam Dell, 2008, p. 40.

10. Quoted in Julie Steenhuysen, "Scientists Discover How BRCA-1 Gene Causes Cancer," Reuters, December 9, 2007. www.reuters.com/article/healthNews/idUSN0935659520071209.

11. Rosy Daniel, *The Cancer Prevention Book—A Complete Mind/Body Approach to Stopping Cancer Before It Starts*. Alameda, CA: Hunter House, 2002, p.1.

Chapter Two: Detecting and Diagnosing

12. James Thompson, "Men Get Breast Cancer, Too!," Breast Cancer Stories, March 2, 2004. www.breastcancerstories.org/chapter/71.

13. Quoted in "Breast Cancer Tests: Screening, Diagnosis, and Monitoring," BreastCancer.org, February 10, 2017. www.breastcancer.org/symptoms/testing/types/.

14. Quoted in "Mammography: Benefits, Risks, What You Need to Know," BreastCancer.org, June 14, 2016. www.breastcancer.org/symptoms/testing/types/mammograms/benefits_risks.jsp.

15. Quoted in Rachel A. Clark, MS, Suzanne Snedeker, PhD, and Carol Devine, PhD, "Estrogen and Breast Cancer Risk: The Relationship," Cornell University Program on Breast Cancer and Environmental Risk Factors, March 1998, updated August 16, 2001. envirocancer.cornell.edu/FactSheet/General/fs9.estrogen.cfm.

Chapter Three: Fighting the Good Fight

16. "Treatment and Side Effects," BreastCancer.org. www.breastcancer.org/treatment/.

17. Quoted in "Stages of Breast Cancer," BreastCancer.org, January 26, 2017. www.breastcancer.org/symptoms/diagnosis/staging.jsp.

18. Quoted in "How Radiation Works," BreastCancer.org, January 4, 2016. www.breastcancer.org/treatment/radiation/how_works.jsp.

19. Jeannette, "Jeannette's Story," BreastCancerStories.org, January 9, 2008. www.breastcancerstories.org/chapter/153.

Chapter Four: Surviving Breast Cancer

20. Kimalea Conrad, "Kimalea Conrad—Breast Cancer Survivor," Cancer Treatment Centers of America, 2017. www.cancercenter.com/community/survivors/kimalea-conrad/.

21. Ellen H. Zahlis and Frances M. Lewis, "Coming to Grips with Breast Cancer: The Spouse's Experience with His Wife's First Six Months," *Journal of Psychosocial Oncology*, vol. 28, no. 1, 2010. www.ncbi.nlm.nih.gov/pmc/articles/PMC2856107/.

22. Quoted in "Is Mastectomy Right for You?," BreastCancer.org, January 15, 2015. www.breastcancer.org/treatment/surgery/mastectomy/who_for.jsp.

23. Lauren Alix Brown, "New Research Shows that Mastectomy Is Better for Young Women with Early Stage Breast Cancer," Quartz, May 3, 2016. qz.com/674567/new-research-shows-that-mastectomy-is-better-for-young-women-with-early-stage-breast-cancer/.

24. Quoted in Eun Kyung Kim, "Meet the Tattoo Artist Making Breast Cancer Survivors Feel 'Whole Again,'" *Today*, October 20, 2016. www.today.com/health/meet-tattoo-artist-making-breast-cancer-survivors-feel-whole-again-t48276.

25. Quoted in Marie McCullough, "Younger Women with Breast Cancer Increasingly Choose Double Mastectomies, Study Finds," Philly.com, March 29, 2017. www.philly.com/philly/health/breastcancer/Young-women-with-breast-cancer-increasingly-choose-double-mastectomies-study-finds.html.

26. Quoted in "Chemotherapy Side Effects," Breast Cancer.org, February 14, 2017. www.breastcancer.org/treatment/chemotherapy/side_effects.jsp.

27. Quoted in Samantha Critchell, "Campaign Aids Cancer Patient Beauty Routine," *Springfield News-Leader*, October 16, 2009, p. 4C.

28. Quoted in Critchell, "Campaign Aids Breast Cancer Patient Beauty Routine."

29. Quoted in "Getting the Support You Need," Breast Cancer.org, May 2, 2017. www.breastcancer. org/symptoms/types/recur_metast/living_metast/ support.jsp.

30. Quoted in "If Cancer Comes Back," BreastCancer. org. www.breastcancer.org/symptoms/type/recur_ metast/fear_combk.jsp.

31. Robyn Wolfe, "Standing Up to Cancer," *Today*, last updated July 8, 2013. www.msnbc.msn.com/ id/33245310.

Chapter Five: For the Future

32. Quoted in Kristina Fiore, "Smoking Causes Breast Cancer, Analysis Shows," MedPage Today, April 24, 2009. www.medpagetoday.com/ PrimaryCare/Smoking/13899.

33. Quoted in "Locally Advanced Breast Cancer More Deadly in Obese," Caring4Cancer, March 14, 2008. www.caring4cancer.com/go/multiplemyelo- ma/news?NewsItemId=20080314elin013.xml.

34. Quoted in Charnicia Huggins, "Diet Plus Ex- ercise Up Survival After Cancer," Reuters, June 21, 2007. www.reuters.com/article/ healthNews/idUSCOL15786220070621.

35. Quoted in Aine Fox, "Breast Cancer Treatment Breakthrough After 'Milestone' Genetic Discov- ery," *Independent*, May 2, 2016. www.independent. co.uk/life-style/health-and-families/health-news/ breast-cancer-treatment-breakthrough-after-mile- stone-genetic-discovery-a7010521.html.

36. Elaine Schattner, "MammaPrint, Agendia's Breast Cancer Test, Is Having a U.S. Moment. Can It Reduce Overtreatment?," *Forbes*, April 21, 2016. www.forbes.com/sites/elaineschat- tner/2016/04/21/mammaprint-a-molecular-breast- cancer-test-is-having-a-moment-early-mindact- trial-results/#303e024a5b39.

37. Elisa Port, *The New Generation Breast Cancer Book.* New York, NY: Ballentine Books, 2015, pp. ix-x.

angiogenesis: The process in which a tumor creates new blood vessels for itself.

axilla: The armpit.

digital tomosynthesis: A diagnostic test that uses X-rays to create a three-dimensional view of the breast.

ducts: The tiny tubes inside the breast that carry milk to the nipple.

lobules: Collections of tiny sacs inside the breast that produce and secrete milk.

margins: The edges or ends of a piece of tissue that have been surgically removed; the margins are checked for cancer cells to make sure that all the cancer has been removed.

metastasis: The spread of cancer from its original location to other organs or bones.

mutation: A change, or error, in a gene that causes it to malfunction.

oncology/oncologist: The study of cancer, its causes, diagnosis, and treatments. An oncologist is a physician who specializes in oncology.

palpation/palpable: A method of identifying potential problems in a body part using gentle pressure with the hands; a mass that can be felt with the fingers is said to be a palpable mass.

***peau d'orange*:** A French phrase meaning "orange peel skin;" a skin condition in which the skin has a thickened, puckered appearance similar to the peel of an orange.

targeted therapy: A precise method of cancer treatment that uses drugs designed to target only cancer cells and not healthy cells.

After Breast Cancer Diagnosis (ABCD)
5775 N Glen Park Road, Suite 201
Glendale, WI 53209
(414) 977-1780, or support helpline (800) 977-4121
www.abcdbreastcancersupport.org
abcdinc@abdcmentor.org
Founded by breast cancer survivors, ABCD works one-on-one with patients, families, and friends. Its goal is to decrease the impact of breast cancer on women and families by providing information, increasing awareness, and helping ensure that no woman has to face breast cancer alone.

American Breast Cancer Foundation (ABCF)
10400 Little Patuxent Parkway, Suite 480
Columbia, MD 21044
(410) 730-5105
www.abcf.org
info@abcf.org
The mission of the ABCF is to provide education, emotional and financial support, and early detection screening services to low-income, rural communities in the United States.

American Cancer Society (ACS)
250 Williams Street NW
Atlanta, GA 30303
(800) 227-2345
www.cancer.org
The ACS works for cancer treatment, prevention, and quality of life issues through research, education, patient services, and rehabilitation. Its website features news and information, message boards, links to its programs (including Reach to Recovery), and live chat.

CancerCare
275 Seventh Avenue
New York, NY 10001
(800) 813-4673
www.cancercare.org
info@cancercare.org
CancerCare offers education, emotional support, information, and practical help to people with cancer and their families. Specialists are available for personal phone consultations.

National Breast Cancer Coalition (NBCC)
1010 Vermont Avenue NW, Suite 900
Washington, DC 20005
(800) 622-2838
www.breastcancerdeadline2020.org
info@breastcancerdeadline2020.org
The NBCC works to promote increased funding for breast cancer research at national, state, and local levels and works with scientists to improve diagnosis, treatment, and access to high-quality care. It has recently set a goal to end breast cancer by 2020.

The Susan G. Komen Breast Cancer Foundation
5005 LBJ Freeway, Suite 250
Dallas, TX 75244
(877) 465-6636
komen.org
helpline@komen.org
Founded by Nancy Brinker to honor her sister, Susan G. Komen, who died of breast cancer in 1980, this nonprofit organization works through a large network of volunteers in local chapters throughout the United States. Its mission is to eliminate breast cancer as a life-threatening disease through research, education, screening, and treatment.

Books

Bryfonski, Dedria. *Breast Cancer*. Farmington Hills, MI: Greenhaven Press, 2016.
This book presents opposing viewpoints on many aspects of breast cancer, allowing the reader to think critically about the issues.

Parks, Peggy J. *Breast Cancer*. San Diego, CA: ReferencePoint Press, 2014.
This short reference book provides as overview of breast cancer, what causes it, and prevention and treatment.

Rauf, Don, Alvin Silverstein, Virginia B. Silverstein, and Laura Silverstein Nunn. *What You Can Do About Breast Cancer*. New York, NY: Enslow Publishing, 2016.
The authors discuss what breast cancer is as well as the latest research and treatments.

Silver, Maya, and Marc Silver. *My Parent Has Cancer and It Really Sucks*. Naperville, IL: Sourcebooks Fire, 2013.
This resource for teenagers who have had a parent diagnosed with cancer includes stories from teens across the country and information from medical professionals.

Weiss, Marisa C., and Isabel Friedman. *Taking Care of Your "Girls": A Breast Health Guide for Girls, Teens, and In-betweens*. New York, NY: Three Rivers Press, 2008.
This book educates young girls about their breasts—development, self-image, clothing, and health.

Websites

BreastCancer.org

www.breastcancer.org

This extremely comprehensive website offers a wealth of information on all aspects of breast cancer.

Breast Cancer Prevention Partners

www.bcpp.org

This resource focuses on ways to prevent breast cancer and on how the environment affects the human body.

Center for Young Women's Health

www.youngwomenshealth.org

This website gives information for teenage girls about health and development. It also provides an educational page about the important routine of breast self-exams under the General Health section.

Mayo Clinic

www.mayoclinic.org

One of the nation's leading health care centers offers important information about breast cancer.

National Breast Cancer Foundation, Inc.

www.nationalbreastcancer.org

This website provides information and help for those coping with breast cancer.

INDEX

A
American Association for Cancer Research, 85
American Cancer Society, 22, 25, 52, 72, 77
Anderson Cancer Institute, 25
anesthesia, 35, 39, 44–45, 48, 58, 62
antiemetics, 66
anxiety, 9, 49, 70
Ashkenazi Jewish descent, 7
axillary nodes, 21, 46, 48–49, 55, 64

B
benign tumor, 13–14
bilateral mastectomy, 55
biopsy, 31, 33, 36, 45, 47, 74
blood changes, 66
bone density, 66
bone scan, 41, 74
Boughey, Judy C., 63
brachytherapy, 54–55
BRCA, 23–25, 83, 88
breast exam, 32–33
breastfeeding, 16, 64, 79
breast implants, 59, 61, 63, 73
breast self-exam (BSE), 28, 32

C
calcifications, 30
carcinoma, 14, 17–18
Centers for Disease Control and Prevention (CDC), 7, 81
chemotherapy-induced nausea and vomiting (CINV), 66
chromosomes, 12, 23
clinical trial, 76–78
coma, 14
complete blood count (CBC), 39
computer-aided detection and diagnosis (CAD), 31
computerized tomography (CT) scan, 39–40, 74
core biopsy, 34
Cornell University, 36
cyst, 6, 30, 33

P

Paget's disease, 19
pain medication, 45, 64, 75
Pantene Beautiful Lengths, 67
pathologist, 35
patience, 19
peau d'orange, 19
Pierce, John, 81
platelets, 39, 68
poly ADP-ribose polymerase (PARP) inhibitors, 88
Port, Elisa, 88
positron emission tomography (PET) scan, 40, 74
pregnancy, 24, 36, 68–69
progesterone, 36–37
prosthetics, 58, 62
PTEN, 23

R

radiation, 9, 22, 24, 30, 43–45, 47–49, 53–55, 57–58, 65, 69–70, 74, 78, 88
Reach to Recovery, 72
reconstructive surgery, 47, 58–59, 62–63
recurrence, 30, 39, 51, 57, 73–75, 81, 86
red blood cells, 39, 68
Reville, Barbara, 66
risk factors, 22, 24–26, 29, 79, 81–82

S

scintimammography, 82
Scotland, 8
self-conscious, 65
sentinel node biopsy, 47–48
skin fibroma, 13
skin irritation, 69
skin tag, 13
smoking, 25–26, 79
Solin, Lawrence
    on advance of tissue-sparing lumpectomy, 9
    on early detection, 11
Spot-Light HER2 CISH test, 84
Stage I breast cancer, 20, 22
Stage II breast cancer, 20, 22
Stage III breast cancer, 21–22, 53, 75
Stage IV breast cancer, 21–22, 53

stem cells, 86
support, 27, 55–56, 62, 70–73, 75
surgical biopsy, 34–35, 44, 74
Susan G. Komen Breast Cancer Foundation, 27
swelling, 19, 49, 65, 70, 75

T

Tamoxifen, 52
tattoos, 60, 63
tenderness, 59, 70
three main categories of breast cancer tests, 29
tissue flap reconstruction, 60
TPIV 110, 78
transverse rectus abdominis muscle (TRAM) flap, 61

U

underdiagnosis, 38

V

vaccines, 78
vascular endothelial growth factor (VEGF), 37

W

weakness, 48, 50, 68
Weiss, Marisa, 43, 53
Wellcome Trust Sanger Institute, 84
what not to say to someone with breast cancer, 62
white blood cells, 16, 67, 70
Wigs for Kids, 67
Women's Health and Breast Cancer Right Act of 1990, 60

X

X-rays, 19, 27, 39–40, 74, 83

Y

yoga, 49

ABOUT THE AUTHOR

Michelle Denton received her bachelor's degree in English and creative writing from Canisius College in 2016, graduating cum laude from the All-College Honors Program. She lives in Buffalo, New York, with her mother and two cats, and she has made writing her full-time career. She also works as props master and sometimes-stage manager at the Subversive Theatre Collective, and she is currently trying to find the time to write her first novel.